INDESTRUCTIBLE

INDESTRUCTIBLE

BLAKE K. HEALY

CHARISMA
HOUSE

Most Charisma House Book Group products are available at special quantity discounts for bulk purchase for sales promotions, premiums, fund-raising, and educational needs. For details, call us at (407) 333-0600 or visit our website at www.charismahouse.com.

Indestructible by Blake K. Healy
Published by Charisma House
Charisma Media/Charisma House Book Group
600 Rinehart Road, Lake Mary, Florida 32746

Visit the author's website at blakekhealy.com.

Library of Congress Cataloging-in-Publication Data

Names: Healy, Blake K., author.
Title: Indestructible / by Blake K. Healy.
Description: Lake Mary, Florida : Charisma House, 2020.
Identifiers: LCCN 2019049414 (print) | LCCN 2019049415 (ebook) | ISBN
    9781629996776 (trade paperback) | ISBN 9781629996783 (ebook)
Subjects: LCSH: Spiritual warfare. | Angels. | Demonology.
Classification: LCC BV4509.5 .H425 2020 (print) | LCC BV4509.5 (ebook) |
    DDC 235/.4--dc23
LC record available at https://lccn.loc.gov/2019049414
LC ebook record available at https://lccn.loc.gov/2019049415

Some names in this book have been changed to protect the privacy of those
individuals. Any similarity between the names and stories of individuals
described in this book and individuals known to readers is purely
coincidental.

While the author has made every effort to provide accurate internet
addresses at the time of publication, neither the publisher nor the author
assumes any responsibility for errors or for changes that occur after
publication. Further, the publisher does not have any control over and does
not assume any responsibility for author or third-party websites or their
content.

20 21 22 23 24 — 7 6 5 4 3
Printed in the United States of America

CONTENTS

INTRODUCTION

I COUNTED AT LEAST fifteen angels in the church sanctuary. I could see a few more through the window to the foyer but figured that it would be best to keep it simple and focus on the room that I was in. I flipped open my notebook and started jotting down a brief description of each angel.

They seemed to be arranged in three groups of five. One group stood on the stage where the band was preparing to start the worship service. The other two groups were on the ground in front of the stage, one to the far right, the other to the far left. All the angels were wearing white robes with gold stitching. All were different sizes but within the boundaries of average human height. All except one.

One of the angels stood at the very center of the stage. This angel was easily nine feet tall with bright golden hair that matched his broad, golden wings. The other angels were standing casually, arms at their sides. This angel stood with his arms outstretched, eyes gazing upward with intense, childlike wonder.

The tall angel brought his arms down in a swift motion, somewhere between that of a conductor leading a symphony and a general adding emphasis to a command. All at once the angels on and at either side of the stage snapped into a clear formation, and the band struck the first note of the first worship song.

The tall angel returned to his worshipful stance, arms out, eyes up. The other angels on stage followed suit as the angels on the ground began to dance. They ran up and down the aisles with great leaping steps that would have made even the most talented ballet dancer look clumsy. Each leap grew longer and longer as the song continued, and a soft greenish mist began to fill the room. With it came the distinct sensation of peace that I associated with the presence of God.

My eyes bounced back and forth between the angels and my notes as I did my best to scribble down as much detail as I could manage without getting too far behind. I took in a deep breath and gave my stiff fingers a stretch. I looked around at the rest of the room and felt my heart sink. There was so much that I wasn't writing down.

Each person in the room had a personal angel standing near him or her, each of which was participating with worship in a unique way: dancing, singing, jumping up and down. The green mist was wrapping around people in the room like a warm blanket. Heavy chains that had been hanging across some people's shoulders began falling to the ground in response to the mist.

About a dozen different demons were spread across the

room. Each was gray-skinned, bony, and under three feet tall and only vaguely resembled the shape of a human. They had been wandering around the room like someone having a hard time finding an open seat but were now shying away from the mist as if it was dangerous to breathe.

There was so much that I didn't have time to write down. I was barely able to keep up with what the angels were doing in conjunction with worship. I snapped the notebook shut, dropped it to the ground next to my feet, and let out a heavy sigh.

I was fourteen years old. Though I had been seeing angels, demons, and other spiritual things for as long as I could remember, it had been only two years since I learned that my open visions were the result of a God-given gift. Though I had grown up in a Christian family, the churches we attended did not teach about spiritual gifts or seeing in the spirit realm, so I never had a clear context for the things I saw. My whole world changed when we started attending a church that was very active about training its congregation in the gifts of the Spirit.

Though none of the leaders at the church saw in the spirit the way that I did, they all did their best to help me steward and grow my gift. Recording the things I saw in a notebook had been one of their suggestions. I had been keeping this habit sporadically for the last two years. It was days like this that made it easy to be sporadic. I wanted to help and bless others with the things I saw, but it was hard to know how to do that when there was so much to see. Which things were most important? Which would be most helpful?

I looked down at the notebook, gave a frustrated grunt, and picked it back up. Better to write down something than nothing, even if it was less than a tenth of what was happening. I decided to just focus on what the angels were doing in response to worship.

The large angel on the stage was now floating several feet above the ground, waving its arms in wide wind-mill patterns. It still had the same expression of childlike wonder and delight shining on its face. The smaller angels on stage followed the larger angel's lead, their rhythm and motion complementing the movements of the larger angel. The dancing angels were still bounding up and down the aisles, but their leaps had grown so large that some of them bounded from the back of the room to the front of the stage in a single leap.

Whether it was because of what the angels on the stage were doing, the way the angels in the aisles were dancing, or something else entirely, the green mist in the room began to swirl. It churned in a great swell, rushing forward from the stage, crashing into the back wall, flowing upward and across the ceiling, then back down to the stage again like the spin cycle of a giant washing machine.

The mist rushed through the congregation faster and faster, blowing away dust and dirt that had been so fine that I hadn't noticed its presence until it was gone. I began to feel an electric heat build in my chest as the intensity of the music rose to match what was happening in the spirit. All the people in the room began glowing brighter and brighter as if the movement of the mist was polishing them, making them shine. Soon the brightness became so intense that I had to stop looking in the spirit. Instantly the swirling mist and dancing angels vanished. The sudden switch made the room seem empty, but the rising heat in my heart reminded me that everything that I had seen was still happening.

After worship was over, while someone stepped onto the stage to go over the morning's announcements, I sat down to fill in extra notes on the things I had seen. I had scribbled down only a bare-bones account of the angels and what they were doing. I had not had time to add any further thoughts.

Remembering how the other angels had seemed to defer to the larger angel, I wrote down, "Worship leader angel?" next to my description of the angel with golden wings. I also included, "Childlikeness, childlike faith, wonder," while remembering the expression that was on the angel's face all during worship. Next to the description of the green mist I wrote, "Presence? Presence of God? Wind of the Spirit?"

As I was thinking about how the demons had shied away from the mist and was wondering how they had responded when the mist started swirling, the person on stage announced that all children and youth were released to go to their classes. I quickly jotted down, "Scared them away," and tossed my notebook into my backpack.

The church owned two buildings separated by a parking lot. One building housed the sanctuary and children's classrooms, and the other held the administrative offices and the room where the youth met. I pushed through the sanctuary doors and started the trek across the parking lot toward the other building with the twenty or so other kids who were in the youth group. I trailed at the back of the group, my thoughts still on what I had seen during worship.

Though seeing in the spirit came as naturally to me as seeing everything else, understanding the things that I saw was an entirely different matter. Some of what I saw was straightforward and intuitive. An angel dancing during a worship service is probably worshipping. An angel standing at attention near a doorway, weapon in hand, is probably a protection angel. Other things, like the green mist I had seen earlier, were not so clear cut. I could feel the meaning behind it, but like a forgotten word at the tip of my tongue, I couldn't put language to that meaning.

I looked up at the trail of kids on their way over to the youth building. Each was still glowing from what had happened during the final few moments of worship. Words like *refining*, *blessed*, and *presence* came to mind, but none felt more accurate than the others. I was rolling this over in my mind, feeling mildly frustrated at being unable to assemble anything useful out of my thoughts, when I was struck with a sudden sense of foreboding.

A heaviness came over me, starting at the top of my head and running down to my shoulders, causing me to look up. Though it was a bright and sunny California day, what I saw in the sky made it seem darker than if it had been filled with rain clouds. A massive bird with scraggly black feathers and a hooked beak was circling just above the parking lot. The distance made it hard to judge, but at first glance it seemed to have at least a twenty-foot wing-span. I didn't know enough about birds to judge whether it looked more like a hawk or a falcon, but even to my inexperienced eye it was clear that this was a predator.

I immediately recognized the large bird as a principality, a demonic entity that seeks to influence a city or region, and though I had seen others like it on numerous occasions, I had very little understanding of what these large bestial beings did, apart from the few references to them I had read in the Bible. This was not the first time I had seen this massive bird. It had been flying above the region for as long as I had lived there, so what sent chills down my spine was not its presence but the fact that it was, unmistakably, staring right at me and the other youth kids.

Its gaze shifted from one kid to the next, a predator selecting its prey. I watched in chilled silence as its eyes passed over me and then locked on two girls who were walking a few yards in front of me. Images flashed through my mind in rapid succession: a shouting match between children and parents, kids running away from home, drug abuse, homelessness, sickness, sorrow. Each image swept through my mind in less than a tenth of a second, blurry and distorted, but each was laced with the pain of watching someone's life fall apart. The helpless dread built to a peak, then the massive bird arched into a dive.

I wanted to shout out a warning, but my lips wouldn't move. I wanted to run and push them out of the way, but my legs were frozen. It was taking longer than I expected for the beast to reach the ground; it had been much higher than I had guessed. I realized, as it came plummeting to the earth, that it was more than twice as large as I had expected, maybe even larger than that.

Tears began forming in the corners of my eyes as I looked down at the two girls, ignorant of their peril, giggling in casual conversation as they crossed the parking lot.

The great black bird came down in a blur, wings arched back, beak pointed like the tip of a spear directly at the girls. One of the girls must have said something funny, because moments before impact, both girls reared back their heads and let out a burst of uncontained laughter. Everything happened so fast that I could not be entirely certain of the order in which it happened. The bird fell faster than a meteor, the girls laughed, there was a blinding flash of pale green light, and the monstrous bird slammed into the light like it was forty inches of hardened steel. It ricocheted somewhere behind me in a broken heap.

The paralyzing dread melted away so thoroughly that it instantly felt like a distant memory. The girls continued walking and talking cheerfully, showing no sign of recognition of what had just happened. I stood in stunned astonishment, turning just in time to see the principality flying off into the distance. The beat of its wings was stuttered and arrhythmic, compensating for damaged tendons and cracked bones.

I shook my head, trying to sort what I had seen. I could remember the fear that I felt, but with the feeling gone, I was hard pressed to understand why I had felt so severely afraid. It seemed silly, even in such recent retrospect. I could not figure out why this principality had decided to attack today of all days. Was it the girls' conversation that repelled the demon? Was it what had happened in worship?

I fumbled my notebook free of my backpack and scribbled a messy account of what I had seen. I looked up as I finished and realized that almost all the other kids had already entered the youth building. I moved to follow them but then stopped and quickly wrote down one last thought: "It really seemed like the laugh is what did it." Then I threw the notebook into my backpack and jogged to catch up to the others.

HOW TO WIN

I have always had a hard time talking about demons. This is not because they are too frightening or because I am worried about some kind of backlash; it is because most people are either so frightened by the topic that they would rather avoid it completely or so focused on it that I am hesitant to stoke the fires of their fixation. Also, I find it difficult to give attention to the plans and purposes of the enemy when there are so many plans and purposes of heaven to be seen. For these and other reasons that I will discuss in greater detail later in this book, I have spoken very little about demons, especially in recent years.

"But it would just be so helpful to know. It would be so much easier to guard ourselves if we knew what the enemy was doing. It would help us know how to pray," is usually what people say when trying to press me to talk more about the demonic. And while some part of me always agreed,

I was rarely pleased by the fruit produced by indulging these questions. Talking about the demonic almost always left people afraid or overly focused on darkness.

Indestructible is my third book about seeing in the spirit. My first book, *The Veil*, was about how I came to understand the things that I see and the purpose behind them. My second book, *Profound Good*, was about how the gift of seeing in the spirit is designed to invite us into a deeper and more personal relationship with God and how every Christian can pursue this gift for himself or herself.

In *The Veil* I included only as many stories about demons as were necessary to create a clear picture of how the spirit realm works and to address some of my early experiences before I understood this gift. *Profound Good* had even fewer references to the demonic, focusing almost entirely on God and His goodness. In the middle of my preparation to write that book, the Lord spoke to me.

"I want you to write a book about spiritual warfare," He said.

"Oh no," I responded, pressing a palm to my forehead, "anything but that."

He did not respond to my objection.

"But there are already so many books about spiritual warfare," I said, scrambling for an excuse. "There are tons of really good ones."

"I want you to write your book on spiritual warfare," He said, putting heavy emphasis on *you* and *your*.

"But it never helps. It scares people. It freaks them out or weirds them out or tweaks them."

"It won't."

Memories began to flood my mind as He spoke the last two words. I saw all the times I tried to tell people about demons I saw on or around them. I remembered the looks of fear, pain, and confusion it had caused. I saw flashes of every reason I had stopped talking about demons. Then I felt the presence of God weave into my memories, turning them to visions of an alternate past.

Instead of expressions of fear and confusion, the people wore looks of confidence and relief. Their eyes lit up. They stood up straight. The presence of God surrounded them more fully. Shackles fell from their wrists. Cuts and bruises faded away. They were becoming whole.

I felt tears start to form as I saw picture after picture of the freedom I had never been able to impart but had always hoped to. For thirty years I had watched people suffer at the hands of the enemy. I watched people fall prey to the same traps over and over again, be baited into needless bitterness, spend decades battling a meaningless, paper-thin lie, and be tricked into believing in a carefully crafted illusion, and nothing I said ever seemed to help.

"I want you to write a book about spiritual warfare," He said, more gently this time. "I want you to tell them how to win."

"OK," I said, wiping the tears from my face. "What do You want me to say?"

HOW TO GET THE MOST OUT OF THIS BOOK

This book represents the sum of thirty years of observing the plots of the enemy and the plans of heaven. My goal is to teach you how to understand and outmatch the former while becoming a champion of the latter.

To this end, here are a few notes to help you get the most out of this book:

1. This is not a book about demons.

While the Holy Spirit has corrected me about avoiding the subject of demons because of the confusion and fear it can cause, my conviction that our focus should always be on the things of heaven has not wavered in the slightest. All accounts and details regarding the demonic in this book exist to help you avoid anything that would delay or distract you from growing in relationship with your heavenly Father and from releasing His kingdom across every part of the earth.

2. Do not be afraid.

One of the most common tactics of the enemy is to perpetuate the lie that it is better/safer/easier to remain ignorant of the demonic. The truth is that the things recounted in this book are happening whether we are aware of them or not. Ignorance neither protects nor preserves us. The deeper truth is that when we view the demonic from heaven's perspective, then fear is no longer part of the equation. If we do not take the risk of trying to look from God's perspective at the things we fear, then we rob ourselves of the opportunity to grow our faith. You do not need to be brave; you need only to know who is with you.

3. You are going to have to change.

It may seem presumptive or harsh, but in my experience, growth and change are a fundamental part of seeing the kingdom of God manifest in your life. Some of you will need to change the way you think. Some of you will need to change the way you act. Some of you will need to change the way you believe. These are not changes that will earn you the blessings of heaven; the blood of Jesus has already won those for you. But they will equip you to receive and bear that blessing.

In this book you will find areas where you are strong. You will also find areas where you are weak. To help with this, I am recommending additional resources on each topic we discuss. If you should find a need for personal growth in a particular chapter or paragraph, then please pursue the recommended material. Others have much deeper revelation than I do on some of these topics, and I encourage you to pull from their strength. They have all been a great source of growth for me.

Lastly, I would like to make a quick note on the structure of this book. I have endeavored to compile what I have learned about spiritual warfare after over thirty years of seeing in the spirit. To communicate all this as clearly and concisely as possible, I have broken the subject into four broad topics.

Part 1, Context and Fundamentals, covers some of my personal history with spiritual warfare as well as some of the fundamentals that help us understand what kind of war we are fighting and what kind of war we are not fighting.

Part 2, Tactics and Traps, outlines many of the ways the enemy tries to attack and deceive God's people. Here you will find many stories of the kinds of things I have seen the enemy bring against people as well as some ways to recognize if you are under this kind of attack.

Part 3, Becoming Indestructible, addresses not only how we can repel the attacks of the enemy but also how we can build our lives in such a way that his attacks have little or no effect on us.

Part 4, The Winning Side, illustrates how we can take an offensive stance in our spiritual warfare—not just rebuffing the attacks of the enemy but releasing God's kingdom on the earth.

While I do think that these aspects of spiritual warfare are deeply dependent on one another and essentially part of the same whole, I think that we can better understand how they work together by separating them and taking a deeper look at each.

I hope that in doing this, you will discover that God is not just protecting you; He has equipped you to protect yourself. He is not just advancing His kingdom; He has chosen you to advance it with Him. And you are not just able to survive your time on this planet; you are called to shine.

PART I

CONTEXT AND FUNDAMENTALS

For by him all things were created, in heaven and on earth, visible and invisible, whether thrones or dominions or rulers or authorities—all things were created through him and for him.

—COLOSSIANS 1:16, ESV

MY FIRST TWO books, *The Veil* and *Profound Good*, both focused on the gift of seeing in the spirit. And while this book is, as I have already mentioned, written from the perspective of that gift, it is not about the gift itself. Despite this, I wanted to provide a little practical knowledge on how this gift works so that those who are not familiar with my previous books are not too disoriented and are able to get the most out of this book.

The best language I have found for describing how I interpret the things that I see is that I consider them a literal metaphor. I see angels and demons with my physical eyes, but they are not physical beings. Right now, there is a protection angel standing in the entryway to my house. He is about eight feet tall, wearing leather armor, and holding a long spear. He is lean and muscular, with flecks of gray in his hair and several age lines across his face.

I believe this angel is literally here as a protector, but I do not believe that his protection looks the same as it would if he were physically here. For example, I do not think this angel is standing in my doorway keeping watch for any demons that might try to sneak in when I go get my mail. I do not think, if a demon should come in, that my safety would be a matter of whether this angel could outmatch it in a battle or a test of strength. That is, in my opinion, too literal an interpretation of the spirit.

So, then, why is the angel here at all, and why is it holding a weapon? My front door is the physical entrance to my house; it is not the only entrance, but it is the main one. This is significant physically, and it is significant symbolically. The angel standing there is a statement. My house is protected.

These are just the broad strokes of the relationship between the literal and the metaphorical. All the details matter too. The angel is wearing leather armor, which is light and flexible, a detail that is consistent with how the angel follows me and my family when we travel together. The angel is holding a spear, a long weapon designed to keep the enemy at a safe distance. This detail suggests that the kind of protection the angel is providing keeps the enemy far away. I don't believe that angels age, at least not the same way that we do, so his graying hair and lined face are more a suggestion of experience and maturity than age.

The details grow only more minute from there, from his posture as he is standing to his expression as he looks watchfully into the distance. The point is that, unlike the physical world, these details are not just the arbitrary result of time and circumstance; they are the expression of a spiritual reality. A literal metaphor.

I say this so that, as you read, you will remember to look for the literal as well as the metaphorical. When you read stories of angels and God's presence, look for how the details and circumstances act as an expression of God's nature and kingdom. When you read stories of demons and deception, look for how their actions and appearance give insight into how to avoid their tactics and traps.

The following chapters provide a little background into my experience with seeing in the spirit and spiritual warfare as well as some fundamentals that can help set the tone for how we engage in this battle.

CHAPTER ONE
LIGHT AND DARK

The light shines in the darkness, and
the darkness has not overcome it.

—John 1:5

I HAVE BEEN SEEING angels and demons for as long as I can remember. When I was young, these open visions blended evenly with every other thing I saw. A man walking down the street with a demon on his shoulder didn't stand out as being any more unusual than a man walking his dog. A fifteen-foot-tall angel wearing a tunic of turquoise and gold was no more attention grabbing than a firefighter or police officer in the uniform of his or her trade. Every part of the world, spiritual or otherwise, was just as interesting and new to me.

I saw angels and demons in about equal measure during the early parts of my life, and for a long time, none of the demons I saw caused me any fear or distress. It was as if an invisible barrier stood between me and the things I saw. Seeing a demon was no more frightening than seeing a lion at the zoo through ten inches of glass. Sure, I had some vague understanding that the thing I was seeing was a dangerous predator, but whether it was my child-like inexperience with real danger or the sense of separation caused by the invisible barrier between us, I felt completely safe.

I remember one night when my family and I were driving home from a late church meeting. I was lying down in the back seat looking out the side window at the streetlights whipping by. After a few minutes, a gray-skinned and scraggly creature glided up to the window. It was the size of a large house cat, with bat-like wings and oversized ears. Immediately the demon started banging and scratching at the window with its clawed hands. It hissed so intensely that it left speckles of saliva on the glass.

Though I clearly recognized its actions and demeanor as aggressive, I felt nothing but a vague curiosity as I looked up at the creature. I got bored after a few minutes and went to sleep. The next morning my dad told me about how a drunk driver nearly rear-ended us on the way home, how he had to run a red light to get out of the way, and how fortunate it had been that he had been looking in the rearview mirror in time to see the speeding car.

My parents didn't know about the things I saw. They were devoted Christians and missionaries, but the churches we attended at the time did not believe that the gifts of the Spirit were meant for today. This gave them no reason to look for signs of gifting and gave me no reason to guess that the things I saw were in any way unusual.

This mutual ignorance remained for most of my young life. Not until I turned nine did I start to realize that I was experiencing something others were not.

It started out slowly at first. When a four-year-old says he sees a giant flying dog or dancing golden lady, it earns an indulgent smile from most adults and is greeted by excitement from other four-year-olds. When a six-year-old says it, the smile is less indulgent and the more mature six-year-olds roll their eyes. When an eight-year-old says it, there is no smile and both adults and children ask, "What do you mean?" in a confused tone.

Frequent travels while growing up as a missionary kid had taught me that some things that were perfectly acceptable to do or say in one country were impolite and crass in another. At first, I justified these shifting reactions as a simple cultural misunderstanding. Maybe it was impolite to talk about the golden ladies. Maybe people thought the giant flying dog was embarrassing and it was rude to bring it up.

These justifications seemed flimsy even at the time, but before I could fully put the pieces together, the way I experienced the things I saw completely changed.

I was nine years old, on a night like any other. My mom tucked me into bed, leaving the door cracked open just enough to let a sliver of light shine in from the hallway. After several minutes, just before I closed my eyes, something darkened the light of the doorway.

I sat up on an elbow and turned to look. A shadow slid through the thin opening of the door. It walked past me, along the side of the bed, and stopped at the foot of the bed. Its only defining feature was a pair of milky-white eyes in the middle of its amorphous head. I watched it with more curiosity than concern. Then its white eyes flashed, and I felt fear such as I had never experienced before in my life.

My entire body tensed as I was pinned down to my bed by what felt like a dozen lead blankets. My gaze was locked to the milky eyes of the shadow. Jolts of panic rushed through my body, alternating between hot and cold flashes. I was drowning in absolute terror.

After a long time, struggling against stiff limbs and fried nerves, I managed to roll over onto my belly, breaking the eye contact with the shadow, and fall asleep. When I woke up the next morning, the fear and the shadow were gone.

I saw demons and angels just as I normally did all that next day as I went to school and followed my normal routine. I felt none of the fear that had been so overwhelmingly present the night before. I was beginning to hope that what had happened with the shadow was nothing more than a fluke. Those hopes were dashed when I found it waiting at the foot of my bed later that night.

My mom tucked me in and kissed me good night. The white eyes flashed the moment she left the room, and again, I found myself drowning in a sea of terror. The whole process started over.

A more detailed account of the things I saw in the days and weeks that followed can be found in my first book, *The Veil*. I pulled very few punches in that description, so you are welcome to seek it out if you wish. But I think a simple overview is adequate for our purposes here.

After a few nights, the shadow was replaced by a cavalcade of horrific images—terrifying visions of things more terrible than I had ever seen in my short life. Full, three-dimensional images of violence and depravity danced across my room each night, all more extreme than anything I had ever seen in any movie or book.

I saw horrible things every night, and every night they got worse. It sometimes took me hours to fall asleep. After a while I started getting heart palpitations as soon as I realized the sun was going down. I didn't know if I was going crazy or if I had been randomly selected to have my life ruined by the forces of hell. And, at that point, I did not know which option I preferred.

I was too scared to tell my parents about the things I was seeing, so I just told them that I was having nightmares. They did their best to help me, but nothing worked. No matter what scripture I quoted, no matter what prayer I prayed, no matter what I did, it got worse every night for three and a half years.

BREAKTHROUGH

When I was twelve years old, we started attending a church that encouraged all its members to grow in the gifts of the Spirit, especially prophecy. My mom convinced me to go to one of the prophetic classes. As I heard the teacher describe the different ways we can hear God's voice, I felt as though the sun was finally breaking though after years of nothing but dark thunderclouds.

He talked about how sometimes we hear God's voice like we hear one another but that this was not the only way God spoke. God could speak with pictures in your mind's eye, a still, small voice in your heart, impressions, and open visions.

It was the first time I ever heard anyone describe anything like what I was experiencing. And though nothing the man said brought any clarity as to why I was experiencing nightly torment, it gave me just enough courage to tell my parents the full extent of what had been happening to me for the last three years.

My parents took me to speak with some of the leaders at the church, and though none of them had experienced the same things that I had, they had at least heard of people like me before. I learned for the first time that the things I saw were the result of a God-given gift.

I walked away from the meeting feeling an overwhelming sense of relief. I had all but resigned to the fact that either I was slowly losing my grip on sanity or the devil had decided to ruin my life, only to discover that I had been given a gift. While this understanding brought me more peace than I had felt in years, I discovered the real beauty of this revelation later that night.

I lay down in my bed and watched as all the implements of my suffering returned for their nightly visit. All the shadows and images were just as vivid and frightening in appearance as they had always been, but I immediately realized that something had changed. Every night since my first encounter with the shadow, I had been overwhelmed with fear. Though the things I saw had grown steadily in severity and intensity, the gripping sense of fear that accompanied them had always been the worst part of the process. The ice-cold fear would pound through my veins and shoot through my nerves, making everything I saw feel tangible, personal, and violating. So, you can imagine how shocked I was when the fear that had become such a consistent part of my life completely failed to show up.

The things I saw that first night after my talk with the church leaders were just as horrible and frightening as the things I had been seeing in the weeks prior, but they carried none of the fear that they once had. With the hostile influence of the fear gone, the images had almost no effect on me. What had been an overwhelming kaleidoscope of horror was now no more frightening than a bad puppet show made from outdated Halloween decorations.

The demonic images came every night that week, and every night they bothered me less. After that week they stopped coming entirely. Three and a half years of torment had come to an end, all because of one conversation.

FUNDAMENTAL ONE

I have put a lot of thought into why I went through that season of fear and torment. Was it because I have an important call on my life that the enemy wanted to undermine? Was it because I opened a door that allowed that kind of attack? Was it something about the area I was living in, the church I was attending, or the people around me? With enough digging, I could come up with evidence to support each of these reasons for my season of pain. However, the more I have grown, the more I believe that these are the wrong questions.

When I ask myself if I am being attacked because of the call on my life, then I am tempted to shrink back from that call, afraid of further retribution. I begin to believe that I am putting myself and my family at risk by pursuing the things of God. This is just another lie, a trick to get me to hide. Every human being on this planet has a call of God on his or her life. The enemy is always doing everything he can to undermine that call, whether you are pursuing it or not. The safest place you can possibly be is in the middle of where God has called you to be. In no other place will you be as empowered, equipped, and capable.

When I ask myself if I have opened a door to allow the enemy to attack, then I am tempted to succumb to shame, paranoia, and self-doubt. After scrounging through my life, desperately searching for why this is happening, I begin to doubt my ability to hear God and see what I need to do. I begin to believe that my flaws are insurmountable. This is just another lie. All have sinned and fallen short of the glory of God. You have flaws, even fatal ones, but so does everyone else. God is the only one who can repair our flaws and teach us how to close the unhealthy doors in our lives. Our introspection rarely provides any assistance to the transformative power of His grace. We need to grow and change, but we can do it only with Him.

When I ask myself if the attack is happening because of my environment, my church, or the people around me, then I am tempted to begin harboring bitterness and resentment. Everything that is wrong with my environment and the people in it is suddenly highlighted. I begin to blame everyone and distance myself. This leads to one of the most nefarious of all the enemy's traps: isolation. It is true that there are flaws in your environment, your church, and the people around you. It is also true that God has a plan to release His goodness and glory into your environment, your church, and the people around you.

The enemy steals because he is a thief. He kills because he is a killer. He breaks because he is a destroyer. Focusing too intently on why and how the enemy does what he does leads to endless and fruitless introspection.

I am highlighting this because I want to address one of the fundamental things we must understand if we are going to fight from the winning side.

Fundamental one:
Spiritual warfare is a battle between light and darkness.

This may seem painfully obvious, but I see so many Christians completely miss the powerful implications of this fundamental truth. The Bible uses light as a way of describing God, His kingdom, His purposes, and His children. The Bible uses darkness as a way of describing sin, the enemy, and his plots. The Bible often uses the image of light and darkness to illustrate the interaction between these two forces.

Light and dark are not equal opposites. God and Satan are not in a battle of equal forces. Light does not just have an advantage over darkness. The forces of good are not just stronger, and they do not just outnumber the forces of evil. Darkness is nothing but the absence of light.

When I walk into my office and turn on the light, there is no struggle for the light to dispel the darkness. The darkness does not peel away in layers like a stain being scrubbed from a floor. The darkness does not slowly retreat like a puddle blown by the wind. It is gone when light is present.

The battle is not about whether light can defeat darkness; the battle is about whether the light is on or not.

I experienced darkness for three and a half years. I prayed every prayer I could think of and every prayer my parents suggested. I declared scriptures about strength, protection, and covering. Nothing helped. Why do you think that was?

I thought that either I was going crazy or the devil had decided to ruin my life. I was powerless in both of those belief systems: "Either my mind is betraying me or the devil is attacking me." My prayers and declarations were powerless because I believed I was powerless. I let that belief trick me into hiding what I was dealing with from my parents.

Then I heard a man teach about hearing the voice of

God. God speaks to people? A little light turned on in my brain. It was enough that my belief began to change: "Either I am going crazy, the devil has decided to ruin my life, or this has something to do with what that man was teaching."

It was enough that I finally felt like I could invite others into what was happening. Doing that turned on another light. I learned that there is a spiritual gift called seeing in the spirit realm. Other people have this gift too. Again, my belief changed: "Either I am going crazy, the devil has decided to ruin my life, or I have a gift from God that I have not learned how to use yet." I was completely powerless in the first two mindsets, but the third was different.

The idea that I had a gift that I had not learned how to use yet completely changed my perspective. Instead of worrying about why the enemy was able to attack me, I was thinking about how I could grow in who God created me to be. Instead of worrying about what was wrong with me, I was thinking about how I could start to use the things I saw to bless others.

I still saw demonic things at night after this mindset shift, but all the fear was gone. After a week of stingless and empty attacks, they stopped coming altogether. Why? Because the light was on.

CHAPTER TWO

A BATTLE OF PERSPECTIVE

You are from God, little children, and have overcome them;
because greater is He who is in
you than he who is in the world.

−1 JOHN 4:4, NASB

AFTER THREE AND a half years of torment, confusion,
and pain, I was completely free. I had been seeing
demons and experiencing tremendous fear every night,
but after one conversation, all the fear was gone. A week
later, the demons didn't even bother trying to come. Every
night was peaceful and restful—for six months.

After six months of peace, I laid my head on my pillow
one night and immediately felt that all-too-familiar sense
of fear wash over me like a wave of ice water. I opened
my eyes and saw a shadowy swirl of dark images begin
seeping into my room from all corners. I leaped out of bed,
instantly furious. This had been defeated in my life. I was
a child of God. This was not allowed to happen.

I paced around my room blurting out every declaration, prayer, and scripture that came to mind.

"God has *not* given me a spirit of fear. You do not have permission to disturb my rest or interrupt my sleep. I am a son of God and subject to His protection."

I kicked at the shadows as they continued to seep in. I punched at the air to punctuate each prayer.

I am a mild person by nature, but after experiencing so much freedom, I was not ready to let the enemy take back even a single step of ground. The fear dissipated as I prayed, then returned, then faded, then returned again. The shadows followed the same pattern, pressing in, then reeling back. This continued back and forth, like a spiritual arm-wrestling match, until one o'clock in the morning. Finally, I felt something break, and the fear left along with the swirling shadows. Relieved and exhausted, I fell back into my bed and went to sleep.

The following night I entered my room ready to fight. I lay down, tense and alert, expecting the cold fear to come rushing in at any moment, but it never did. The next night was free of fear, as was the night after that. Another six months went by before the fear returned.

Again, the fear rushed in the moment I lay down to sleep. Again, I leaped out of my bed with righteous fury pulsing through my veins. And again, I prayed and declared until the fear broke during the early hours of the morning.

Another six months went by—no fear. Six months after that—still no fear. I was beginning to think that the fear had finally given up. Until one night, just as I was about to fall asleep, the fear returned. This time, however, my circumstances were a little different.

I had taken a summer job and had to be at work early the next morning. It was already pretty late. I didn't want to stay up until one or two in the morning praying and fighting. I was tired. As the icy fear crept its way up my spine, I rolled over on my other side, closed my eyes, and went to sleep.

I made my way to bed the following night, sure that I would have to fight twice as hard as before. I lay down in bed, tensing with uncomfortable anticipation, but nothing came. No fear, no shadow—there was nothing. The next night was peaceful, as was the one after that. It was another year before the fear made any attempt to return. When it did, I thought back to the last time the fear had come. "Well," I thought, "that way was much easier." So, I just went to sleep. This time the fear was gone for more than two years.

The fear still tries to come back to this day, sometimes twice a year, sometimes once a year. During one stretch, it was gone for five years straight. It usually lasts for only a single night. I get up and pray against it only when it keeps me from falling asleep or lasts more than one night.

I asked the Holy Spirit a question one morning after having spent the majority of the previous night praying and declaring. "Why do I have to fight for it sometimes?"

"What are you fighting for?" the Holy Spirit asked in return.

I was about to say, "To get rid of the fear," but I realized the thought was wrong the moment it formed. God had not given me a spirit of fear. God is light; fear is darkness. Light does not need to fight to get rid of darkness. If I was fighting to chase away fear, then I was fighting the wrong battle.

"I guess I'm fighting to tell myself the truth," I said. "I'm reminding myself of who I am. I'm reminding myself of whom I belong to. I'm fighting to remind myself of my identity."

I felt Him smile.

FUNDAMENTAL TWO

Because of my experiences as a child, I have never really been a fan of scary movies. I let myself be peer-pressured into watching them a few times as a teenager, and I regretted it every time. While the images were always mild compared to the things I had seen as a kid, the kind of fear they evoked was all too familiar. Sometimes movies that were not particularly scary would have a specific moment or sequence that triggered this same feeling of fear. Sometimes things other than movies caused this unexpected trigger. I once ran into an interesting example of this at a theme park.

I was seventeen and living in Southern California. Disneyland was selling annual passes to local residents at a deep discount that year, so my parents bought them for the whole family. I had just gotten my driver's license, and we lived only twenty minutes away from the park. My younger sisters and I took great advantage of this that summer.

Disneyland had many rides and attractions that I loved, but my favorite was the Indiana Jones ride. This ride had everything: car chases, daring escapes, giant animatronics; even the place where you waited in line was beautifully designed. It was awesome. I loved everything about the ride—almost. Near the end was a large animatronic snake, and for some reason this snake triggered that familiar feeling of fear. It was severe enough that every time we came to that part of the ride, I closed my eyes.

We went to Disneyland every week that summer. Even though we usually had only enough time to go for a few hours, every time, I made sure that we rode the Indiana Jones ride, and every time, I closed my eyes when we got to the snake. I felt bothered that something I otherwise found so enjoyable was being tainted by something so simple. The ride had plenty of other spooky elements, and none of them bothered me. Why did this big snake affect me so severely? Every time we were getting on the ride, I told myself that I would keep my eyes open. And every time we would round the final corner, I would see the snake, feel that rush of fear, and clamp my eyes shut.

I knew the ride was fake. I knew the snake was fake. I knew that there was no danger, yet still I was scared every time.

One day we visited Disneyland and went straight to the Indiana Jones ride. It was the middle of the day, so the park was nearly empty. We ran all the way through the line, jumped into our fake jeep, and started the ride. We bounced and bumped our way through the temple as the thematic music accented every twist and turn. Lights flashed and smoke billowed as we narrowly dodged poison darts, eluded venomous spiders, and nearly fell into a fiery volcano. We rounded the corner, and I saw the snake. For the hundredth time I tried to keep my eyes open, and for the hundredth time the familiar rush of fear made me snap my eyes shut.

By this time, we had been on the ride so many times that I knew exactly how long I needed to keep my eyes closed. I sat with my eyes clenched, listening for the familiar swell of adventurous music that signaled we had escaped, when the music slowly faded and the jeep ground to a halt, right in front of the snake. Then all the lights went out—except the light that was pointed at the snake.

Panic shot through me. My heart started beating twice as hard and twice as fast as I opened and closed my eyes. Part of my brain kept insisting, "The ride is just broken; rides always break, and they'll fix it any second," while the other part of my brain was doing everything it could to keep me from screaming. I sat both motionless and spinning, like a car with the gas floored while it is in neutral, for somewhere between thirty seconds and thirty hours.

Then the lights came on. Not the dramatic strobes and colored lights that normally accompanied the ride, but the maintenance lights—large fluorescent lights that hung from the ceiling.

Everything around me looked completely different. I could see all the seams and gaps between the pieces of the set. I could see the track that the jeeps ran along. I could see that the flames in the volcano were pieces of fabric blown by a fan. Then I turned and looked at the snake.

They must have used some kind of special lighting on the snake during normal operation, because in the sterile fluorescent glow of the maintenance lights, the snake looked surprisingly dull. I could see the cracks in the paint. I could clearly see the separation between the chunk of foam rubber that made up its head and the one that made up its body. I could see all the joints and hydraulics through the gap at the base of the snake; they hadn't even been covered, just obscured by the lighting.

My panic vanished so thoroughly that I immediately felt embarrassed for having been so scared. I had, of course, known that the snake was fake. I could have even made a pretty decent guess as to how all the mechanisms beneath the snake worked. But until the moment the lights came on, I had never experienced how the snake worked.

Less than two minutes after they had come on, the maintenance lights blinked out and the dramatic colored lighting returned, accompanied by a theatrical swell of adventurous music. Then the jeep lurched forward along the track. We rode the ride two more times that day, and both times I kept my eyes open the whole time.

Fundamental two:
Spiritual warfare is primarily
a battle of perspective.

If light does not have to fight to dispel darkness, then why do so many Christians experience the negative effects of spiritual warfare? Why do so many Christians feel harassed by the enemy? Why do so many feel powerless?

While many factors can contribute to this, I find that the solution to many of these challenges is rooted in the fundamental truth that spiritual warfare is primarily a battle of perspective. The battle is whether we choose to see things the way God wants us to see them or the way the enemy wants us to see them.

I was frightened of the snake anytime I went on what was otherwise my favorite ride in the park. It triggered feelings of fear that had been a major point of pain in my life. I knew the ride was fake. I knew the snake was a mechanical illusion. But until I experienced the truth behind the illusion, I could not eliminate the fear.

I know it may seem silly, but I have watched so many Christians be knocked around by a similar process. Like in the theme park ride, the enemy wants us to experience our life with all the lighting just right, obscuring all the gaps and cracks in his lies. He tugs on our emotions, heightening and exaggerating them like the adventurous music. He knocks us around like the bumps and turns on the ride, throwing lie after lie at us fast enough that we don't have time to stop and think about how fake each one is. It is not until we stop and turn on the real light—not lights and shadows that are designed to obscure but the light of heaven that reveals all truth—that we can stop trying to fight off the enemy's lies and instead partner with heaven.

KEEPING PERSPECTIVE

I am a fan of history. One piece of history that always pops in my mind whenever I think about spiritual warfare involves a Japanese soldier at the very end of World War II. This particular solider was put in charge of a commando unit that was fighting in the Philippines near the end of the war. He was instructed to undermine the Allied forces in the area by any possible means until he received further instruction.

During this time, the soldier and his unit got cut off from the chain of command. They continued following their orders, undermining and attacking any Allied forces they could find. Shortly after this, the war came to an end. Japan surrendered, but since the soldier and his team were disconnected from any communication, they continued to fight.

This continued for weeks, then months. Local authorities blasted loudspeakers into the jungle where the soldiers were hiding, telling them that the war was over and they could go home. They assumed this was just propaganda, a trick to get them to surrender.

One by one the soldiers died, were captured, or surrendered until only one was left. His surviving comrades wrote notes, explaining that the war had been over for some time now, which were duplicated and air-dropped over the jungle. He assumed that his friends had been forced to write the notes, a trick so that he would be captured as well, so he continued to fight and hide.

Japan surrendered in 1945, but the soldier continued to fight until 1974. A Japanese student who heard the story of this soldier traveled to the Philippines, found the soldier, and convinced him to come home. The soldier agreed on the condition that his commanding officer come and officially relieve him of duty. The student returned to Japan, found the officer, who had long since retired, and returned to the jungle. The soldier was officially relieved of duty and returned home to Japan. He had been fighting in the jungle for twenty-nine years.[1]

I think of this story whenever I think about spiritual warfare because, tragically, I have seen so many Christians make the same mistake. The soldier was cut off from the chain of command. Because of this he spent a huge portion of his life fighting a battle that was already over. I know many Christians who have spent way too much time fighting battles that Jesus already won on the cross. They exhaust themselves fighting for a victory that already belongs to them.

Spiritual warfare is primarily a battle of perspective. If we do not stop and realign our perspective with God's— reconnect with the chain of command—then we run the risk of wasting our time, energy, and pain on a battle that is nothing more than a trick and a lie.

We will be diving into some of the specific tools and lies the enemy uses in part 2 of this book so that you can know what to look for. We will be addressing how we can make ourselves immune to these lies and begin perpetuating the truth in part 3. But for now, know that learning to stop and see things from God's perspective is fundamental to our success in all spiritual warfare.

CHAPTER THREE

HEAVEN'S PERSPECTIVE

Do not be overcome by evil, but overcome evil with good.

—ROMANS 12:21

I SAT IN THE front row of the church, adding the last few details to my notes about what I had seen during worship. There had been only three angels during worship, but they had been running all throughout the room with trains of silver and green cloth so long that they filled the whole room. There had been nearly a dozen angels during the pastor's message, each handing out keys of different sizes to people throughout the congregation.

I looked up and felt the usual dip of disappointment at everything that I had not had time to write down. I was thirteen years old and still discovering how to use the things I saw to help others. The worship team seemed really encouraged when I told them what I saw the angels doing while they were playing. The pastor was always blessed by what was happening in the spirit while he was teaching. But that was only a tiny fraction of what happened in any given church service.

Angels were guarding every entrance and exit. Angels were praying for some people and tending to the wounds of others. Angels were dancing, jumping, and singing, even though there was no music to be heard. Angels were releasing impartations and blessings to dozens of people all across the room while twice as many angels stood waiting for permission to give what they had brought. I was wondering whether these angels were waiting for a signal of permission from God, the people in the room, or something else when a spike of pain shot up my knee.

"So sorry, dear," the old woman said, straightening her walker. "Can't control the darned thing."

"No problem," I said, rubbing the place where the walker had collided with my kneecap.

"Too old to be getting about without breaking something," she said in what was probably supposed to be a joking tone but instead came off as dry and sad.

She shuffled along the aisle, struggling to keep her head high enough to look people in the eye. A demon was lying across her back. It was about the size of a house cat, with black, frog-like skin and an arrogant grin scratched across its face. It was digging an elbow into the nape of her neck, holding her head down. I understood enough about the things I saw to know that the demon was not physically causing her neck to bend. But I had also been seeing long enough to know that there was a connection between her posture and what the demon was doing.

As I looked at the demon, I could feel the same kind of resigned fatalism that I had heard in the woman's half-hearted joke. I could feel the tragedy of lost youth, the resentment of others' vitality, and the empty sorrow of each day being more meaningless than the last. These things were not true, just the lies the demon was telling. She may have been believing all these lies; she may have believed none of them. Guessing by her posture and the wry tone of her joke, I thought she was believing at least a few of them.

I let out a sigh. While I had often told people about the angels that I saw around them, I had not yet tried telling anyone about the demons that I saw. After learning about my gift in the prophetic class, I spent a lot of the first year developing this gift, learning how to focus on different sections of what was happening in the spirit. I practiced focusing on what was happening with individuals, then what was happening corporately; on the good things that were happening, then the bad. Once I was reliably able to do so, I spent most of my time looking at the good. This was partially because I believed that seeing what God was doing was more valuable than seeing what the enemy was doing, partially because there were so many good things to see, and partially because I was scared that I might trigger a repeat of my early childhood experiences.

Watching the old woman scoot her walker across the carpet with her head held low, I realized that if I continued to ignore the demonic, then I was ignoring part of the gift that God had given me. Since I had to learn how to talk about it at one point or another, I might as well start now.

At first I thought about going and telling the woman about what I saw. But I had never spoken to her before the walker incident, and I was not sure if she already knew that I saw in the spirit. I wasn't ready to have the "I've seen in the spirit for as long as I can remember" conversation immediately followed by, "By the way, you have a demon on your neck." Not on my first try, anyway.

I quickly scanned the room, looking for a better candidate. A woman on the far side of the room had a demon on her shoulder. It was stirring a black cloud that hung in the air just above her head. I knew that she had heard me talk about the things I saw at least once before. But she was in the middle of a conversation with someone else, and I did not feel like interrupting.

I spotted a few other possibilities but skipped over each for one reason or another until my eyes locked on a man leaning against the back wall of the sanctuary. A scraggly little demon was floating just above his left shoulder, poking him every few minutes. I had spoken to this man about seeing in the spirit on several occasions, yet still I felt my mind searching for a reason to avoid speaking to him.

Realizing that I was just looking for excuses, I leaped to my feet and started toward him, not wanting my nerves to get the best of me. I took another look at the demon as I approached, wanting to have as much helpful information as I could.

The demon was bony and frail with a bored look on its face. It poked the man with a clawed finger every few minutes, each time in the same place on the side of his head. This must have been happening for a while because there was a small circular scar on the man's temple. Each time the demon poked him, it sent up a little cloud of sickly brown smog that dissipated a few moments after appearing. As I got closer, I could see that there were images in the smog, quick flashes of distinct scenes. Upon seeing them, I realized that I might actually be able to help the man. I took in a deep breath of courage, pressed my nervousness down as low as it would go, and stepped forward.

"Excuse me," I said, trying to speak with as much authority as my thirteen-year-old voice would allow.

"Yes?" he said, looking down at me indulgently. He was probably in his midfifties.

"I couldn't help but notice that you had a demon near your shoulder..." I suddenly did not know if I should describe the whole thing or just get straight to the point. The momentary hesitation had broken the dam on my suppressed nerves, causing a wave of nausea. So I just blurted out, "And I think that maybe you should stop looking at pornography."

His indulgent smile vanished. His face went from pink, to red, to some shade of maroon. He spat out a short series of syllables that sounded more like barks and snarls than words, then stomped out of the room.

A few weeks later, after the sting of my complete and utter failure had faded, I decided to try again. I saw the woman I had seen a few weeks before—the one with a dark cloud over her head. The demon was swirling the cloud, making it bigger, as black rain fell and ran down the woman's face in thick streams. A heavy and familiar fear came over me as I looked at the cloud. This demon was trying to trick this woman into the same kind of fear that I had been trapped in for three and a half years. I knew what that fear was like. I had had victory over that same fear. I knew that I could help.

I walked up to the woman and described what I saw around her. She started crying softly as I spoke.

"Great," I thought, "she is getting breakthrough." So, I described what the fear felt like, hoping this would help her identify it.

Her crying turned to sobbing, with just a little bit of wailing.

"Oh no," I thought, "this is somehow going very badly." I tried to recover by saying that God wanted to take this fear away, that it did not belong to her at all, that she did not need to keep feeling it.

She threw her face into her hands to suppress the growing sobs.

"Wow," I thought, "this is going so much worse than I imagined." I stood there for a while, trying to get her attention with no success. So, I walked away.

Two months and several failures later, a friend of mine from the youth group walked up to me.

"Dude," he said, "you have to tell me if I have a demon on me."

Dread welled up in my chest as each of my many failures passed before my eyes. "No I do not."

"Yes you do. I can totally handle it."

"No you can't," I said. "Nobody can."

We argued for a few minutes before I finally said, "Fine," and looked at him in the spirit.

A small demon was floating in the air just behind his back. It was sickly yellow, vaguely the shape and size of a person, and was made out of something more substantial than cloud but less solid than cotton candy. Regretting that I had agreed to share, I gave him the briefest description I could, and I did not even bother trying to figure out what it was doing or why it was there.

His eyes went wide as saucers as I finished my description. "I knew it."

"What do you mean?" I asked.

Without answering, he slowly turned, eyes still wide, and walked away. He never spoke to me again.

This was the last straw. I wanted to use my gift to help people. People were blessed and encouraged when I talked about seeing angels. Every time I spoke about demons, people were either ashamed, scared, or confused. I decided to stop talking about the demonic entirely. I stuck to this for ten years with only a few exceptions, each of which I regretted.

FUNDAMENTAL THREE

After nearly ten years of avoiding the subject of demons, a longtime friend of mine asked me a question during a walk.

"Blake," she said, "I have been depressed for a month and I don't know why."

"Oh?" I said, looking at the demon that was hovering just over her shoulder.

I was usually pretty good at being subtle about looking in the spirit, but my friend knew me too well. She stopped in her tracks, looked me straight in the eye, and said, "What?"

"What?" I echoed.

She rolled her eyes and took a step forward. "What do you see?"

"See?" I said, trying to raise my shoulders in a way that suggested confusion.

She took another step, stomping her foot just a little harder than she needed to. "Blake, if something is making me depressed, it would help me a lot if you just told me."

Every one of my failures flashed before my eyes. I saw the frightened and confused faces of those who had been hurt by the things I had seen. I felt the anger of everyone who had ever been offended. I remembered the sorrow of having hoped to set people free only to push them deeper into bondage. Then I felt the presence of the Holy Spirit rest on my back like a warm hand. Every fear evaporated, and I knew that it was OK.

"I see a demon," I said. "It's a giant eyeball with a long, sharp nose like a mosquito, little bird legs, and insect wings. It's about as big as a grapefruit."

"Is it my fault that it's here?" she asked. I could feel the vulnerability in her voice.

The Holy Spirit answered her question before she finished asking it; I just repeated the words. "No, but it wants you to think so."

"What do I have to do to make it leave?" she asked, but it was already gone. Believing that it belonged to her was the only thing keeping it there.

Fundamental three:
Seeing the demonic is valuable only when it is seen from heaven's perspective.

Knowledge is powerful. It has the power to build and the power to destroy. During the years that I kept silent about the demonic, one argument would always tempt me to share what I saw. It was some variation of "It would be so helpful to know how I am being attacked." I wanted to help these people, to help them find freedom, but anytime I tried, it led only to more bondage.

My walk with my friend was the first time that I had ever shared about the demonic and felt good about it afterward. The depression she had been stuck under for more than a month completely ended on that day. She felt loved by the Lord, and she did not feel ashamed or exposed in the slightest.

After that conversation I immediately drove home, ran to my room, and pulled out my notebook. I scoured through my notes on other demonic things I had seen, other times I had tried to tell others about what I saw, to find what had been different about this conversation.

As I reviewed my notes and recalled each encounter, I began to see something that had eluded me until that moment. Initially I had been confused when people reacted so badly to my telling them about the demonic. I did not feel any judgment, disvalue, or disgust when I saw the demon near the man with a pornography problem, yet he reacted with such anger and offense. I knew that God was ready to remove the dark cloud over the woman's head just as easily as blowing the steam off a hot cup of tea, yet she was led into deeper despair.

Now that I was older, I could recognize the areas where my poor presentation or lack of tact had contributed to people's reactions, but I had steadily improved in that area while my results remained just as dismal.

Because of this repeated failure, I had abandoned almost all focus on the demonic and committed every bit of energy to learning about how God and His kingdom worked. It turned out that this had been exactly the right thing to do.

I sat on my bed, my notes strewn among my crumpled blankets, thinking about the success I had just had with my friend in the light of all my previous failures.

Again, I felt the gentle touch of the Holy Spirit at my back as He spoke. "I want you to talk more about demons."

The thought was so repugnant to my normal way of thinking that I struggled to not immediately dismiss it. "Why do You want me to do that?"

"Because it will set people free."

Then every moment I had ever seen a demon after I turned twelve years old rushed into my mind—every demon I saw after I learned that what I had was a gift from God. I realized that despite the extreme fear I had experienced when I was young and the occasional nighttime attacks I experienced after that, I was never frightened by what I saw when I was in the Lord's presence. I never felt confused by the demonic things I saw, even when I did not understand them. I never felt disvalue toward others for having demons around them, even when their choices had allowed the demons there. I never felt that any demon I saw was ever more than one moment, one decision, or one word away from being displaced.

The Holy Spirit spoke again as this realization continued to dawn. "I have been training you to see demons the way that I do. I want you to teach others to do the same."

"But I don't know how."

"You don't need to yet. Just watch and I'll show you."

I still didn't talk about demons very much for another ten years, only when the voice of the Holy Spirit was so clear that it would have been direct disobedience to remain silent. I did, however, start looking for them more. I started taking notes on them more. I started having conversations with the Holy Spirit about them more. I started to see the patterns, processes, and principles that became the foundation of the book you are now holding.

Knowledge is powerful. Making sure that you are seeing that knowledge from the right perspective is essential to it being helpful rather than harmful. You may discover that you are being influenced by the demonic. You may discover that this is not your fault at all but a brazen attack. You may find that it is the direct result of your choices. You may find that it is the direct result of others' choices. The enemy will try to double and triple bluff you, lying to you, shaming you for believing a lie, then pointing the finger at others while blowing on the coals of bitterness.

I have seen immensely complicated regimens of lie after lie after lie deposited piece by piece over many years of someone's life, all culminating in a simultaneous detonation of destruction designed to bring that person's entire life crashing down. To sort through the endless wires of deceit coiled through their wounds, mindsets, disappointments, and mistakes that led to such devastation would be nearly impossible. Thankfully, that is not our goal. Our goal is to hear what God has to say about it.

The Bible is full of scriptures encouraging God's children to choose His wisdom over human wisdom. I think that this is just as true with regard to spiritual warfare as it is with any part of life. Sadly, I see so many Christians ignoring the desperate need we have for God's wisdom and perspective regarding spiritual warfare. While it is helpful to understand the plans of the enemy, knowledge of the demonic that is not contextualized by God, His plans, and His nature is always destructive.

The next part of this book contains several descriptions of the kinds of traps and snares that I have seen the enemy lay for God's children. I did not include these so that you can figure them out. I included them so that you can have a spark of recognition in a moment when you are in desperate need of the perspective of heaven. Because seeing the demonic is valuable only when it is seen from heaven's perspective.

PART II
TACTICS AND TRAPS

The thief comes only to steal and kill
and destroy; I have come that they
may have life, and have it to the full.

—John 10:10

MOST OF THE Christians I meet do not know very much
about demons. They believe they exist. They know
that they are bad. That's about it. Some enjoy the distant
comfort of this ignorance, knowing that demons exist but
not really thinking about it long enough to trouble them.
Some are made paranoid by their lack of knowledge, ter-
rified that letting a thought linger or watching the wrong
movie will leave the door open for full demonic assault.
Some let their imaginations fill in the blanks left by their
limited experience, envisioning a world where a demon
can at any moment invade their lives against their wills,
controlling their thoughts and actions.

I hope that in providing this list of tactics and traps,
along with stories that give examples of them, I can help
you begin to fill in your understanding of what demons

do and dispel any false ideas you may have about them. You have probably realized by the tone of the book so far that I have much more value for understanding the things of God than I do for understanding the things of the enemy. I do recognize, however, that a false understanding of how the demonic works can be nearly as destructive as a false understanding of how God works. The simplest framework I can give you for understanding demons is this: demons try to get away with what they can.

The Bible compares the enemy to a roaring lion looking for whom he may devour. The implication is that he cannot just devour anyone; he must look for whom he may devour. Demons are looking for what they can get away with—how big a lie they can get you to believe, how discouraged they can get you to be, how many lies they can get you to believe about yourself, and how many lies they can get you to believe about God. Lies are the only power that demons have, and lies are powerful only if you believe them.

I hope that the following chapters will help you recognize these lies for what they are. I do not like seeing God's children get tricked and ensnared by the tactics and traps of an enemy that has already been defeated.

What follows is information derived from observing the plots and plans of the enemy for more than thirty years. To best illustrate these as clearly and simply as possible, I have split them into a series of short chapters that illustrate and break down these tactics and traps so that you can recognize them if they show up in your own life.

With that said, here are a few keys to help you get the most out of these chapters:

1. The enemy attacks everyone.

I see demons on everyone. If I have not seen a demon on someone, it is because I have not known him or her for very long. Shame about being attacked or allowing yourself to be attacked is one of the primary tactics of the enemy. While it is possible to do things that open you up to attack, the enemy tries to steal from, kill, and destroy all of God's children. It is what he does. You do not need to feel shame because of what the enemy tries to do. You are responsible for how you respond to an attack, not for the action of the attacker.

2. Demons are primarily opportunists.

As you will see in the following chapters, demons are rarely the source of our problems. They are opportunists, scavengers that look for a weakness, wound, or mindset to exploit. Demons cannot control our will or force us to do anything; they cannot force us to make a choice. With that said, they can complicate our decision making by throwing lies into the mix. The following chapters are designed to help you identify when you are under the influence of a lie. The chapters found in part 3 of this book will address how we can shore up our defenses and heal the weaknesses, wounds, and mindsets that attract them.

3. Look for what God is saying.

You will likely find that you have, at one time or another, believed one of these lies or fallen into one of these traps. You may find that you are in the middle of one of them right now. Either way, remember that seeing the demonic is valuable only when it is seen from heaven's perspective. So, if you find yourself stuck in the middle of one of these traps, do not despair and do not become introspective; instead, ask God what He is saying. Trying to get out of a trap on our own leads to exhaustion, causes pain, and is usually fruitless. Letting Him show us how to get out of a trap is much easier and truly liberating.

A FINAL NOTE

You may notice, as you read through these different tactics, that there are no chapters for "The devil ruined my finances" or "The enemy keeps making me sick" or "Satan is making my wife/kids/family/friends hate me."

Life is full of storms, some of our own making and some that seem completely outside our control. In my observation and experience, the real battle begins when we have the opportunity to choose how we are going to respond to the storms of life. This is when the enemy begins throwing these tactics at us, and this is when we get to choose whether we want to fight with the lights on or with the lights off.

You will find more about how to avoid unnecessary storms and how to navigate the storms you cannot avoid in part 3 of this book. In this section we will be addressing how the enemy tries to steer us into needless storms and keep us forever circling in storms we are meant to go through.

CHAPTER FOUR

SHAME

Therefore, there is now no condemnation for those who are in Christ Jesus.

—ROMANS 8:1

I ONCE HAD A friend named Doug. Doug struggled with
substance abuse from a young age, drifting in and out of
rehab like a piece of wood caught by the tide. He stopped
bothering with rehab at twenty-five. By the time he was
thirty, most of the friends who supported his habit had
either gone straight or ended up in prison, so he decided
to do his best to clean up. Over two years he managed to
eliminate all his vices except one: alcohol. No matter what
he tried, no matter how hard he committed, he just could
not let it go.

Doug would do well for weeks or months at a time,
then go on a bender so intense that it was life threatening
to him and terrifying to those who cared about him. A
recent episode had ended with the loss of his license and

a few months in jail. I remember the first time I saw him after he was released.

A demon hovered directly over his head with a big black bucket in its hands. It dumped the bucket over, coating his whole head in thick black oil. Once the bucket was empty, the demon straightened it back up.

"Hey, Doug," I said, shaking his hand. "How's it going?"

"Better than it's been going," he said with half a grin.

The demon tipped the bucket over again, and a fresh batch of oil poured down his face, obscuring it completely.

"I ain't doing that again; I can tell you that much."

A third bucket of oil came pouring down. It was dripping down to his shoes.

"Stupid's got to learn at some point, right?"

Another bucket of oil.

"Least my head isn't thick enough to break rock bottom."

Another.

"Stop!" I said, my voice more panicked than I intended.

He jumped, surprised by my outburst.

"Sorry, I just… you shouldn't talk about yourself that way. You're not stupid at all," I said, sounding as convincing as I could.

"Right." He smiled and patted me on the shoulder. "Nice to see you," he said and walked away.

As I watched him go, I noticed a faint reflection in the dark waves of oil that now covered Doug from head to toe. Images, bent and discolored, glimmered on its surface: Doug drinking; Doug being arrested; Doug in jail; Doug drinking again.

You did not need to see in the spirit to see that Doug felt embarrassed and ashamed at what had happened. But I did notice, as I looked more closely at the distorted images in the oil, that the Doug reflected there did not look like the Doug I knew. The drinking Doug was cavorting around like a maniac, bumping into people, and shouting obnoxiously. The Doug being arrested had a stupid grin on his face the whole time, his features warping in unflattering exaggeration. The Doug in jail looked pathetic and lonely.

I normally don't like using words like *stupid* and *maniac* when describing people, but this is how Doug looked in this twisted version of his memories. The demon was throwing caricatures of Doug's own actions back at him, coating him with shame.

The demon remained over his head for several weeks, dumping the dark oil at regular intervals. After a few weeks, however, things started to change.

I saw Doug one morning and noticed that, though he was still coated in the black oil, the demon above his head did not have a bucket anymore. I was relieved at first, but only for a moment.

The same demon that had been dumping buckets of shame began caressing Doug's face. It rubbed his cheek with an indulgent smile on its face, like it was petting an adorable puppy. I was so surprised and disgusted that it took a few moments before I noticed that the demon was using its other hand to reach a sharp finger toward a wound in Doug's chest.

Wounds are the manifestation of our emotional pain

and trauma. They are the marks that are left behind when people hurt each other with their words and actions or when people hurt themselves with their decisions and thoughts. Not every moment of pain leaves a wound. Most wounds heal before too long, but the ones that don't can cause problems and make us vulnerable to the lies of the enemy.

I watched as the demon tugged at the wound in Doug's chest, causing it to bleed. It moved its hand to his face and started pulling at a scratch on his cheek. The demon found a half dozen more wounds and opened each, all while caressing Doug's face with its other hand. Once all Doug's wounds were bleeding, the comforting hand reached somewhere behind the demon's back and produced a brown bottle. It gently shook the bottle in front of Doug's face.

"How are you doing, Doug?" I asked, trying to sound casual.

"Oh, you know. Fighting the good fight," he answered in a distant voice.

Nothing about Doug's expression showed that he felt any of what was happening, not in the literal sense, but I guessed that he was feeling an all-too-familiar pull to relieve the pain he was feeling.

The next time I saw Doug, he was drunk and trying to hide it. The second Doug saw me, the demon produced a black bucket from behind its back and started pouring the same thick black oil.

I have seen the cycle of shame thousands of times and in a thousand different ways. Stories like Doug's are tragically common, but many shame cycles are much more subtle than his was. I have seen shame dumped on someone who makes a joke that no one laughs at, on someone in the grocery store buying three gallons of ice cream, and on someone showing up late to work.

Guilt and embarrassment are perfectly normal human emotions. We feel guilt when we do something out of alignment with our values. Guilt is useful; it tells us when we are acting differently than we want to. We feel embarrassment when we do something that affects others in a negative way or when we represent ourselves to others in a way that is out of alignment with our values. Embarrassment can be more complicated than guilt, since we want to be careful with how much we let the opinions of others affect our perception of ourselves, but at its root embarrassment is a beneficial emotion that helps us recognize when our actions are affecting others. Shame is not helpful; it is only destructive.

Guilt and embarrassment have to do with how we feel about something we did or thought; shame has to do with what we believe about who we are. Shame attacks our identity. The images of Doug I saw in the black oil made him look stupid, inconsiderate, and pathetic. While Doug's actions could easily be called stupid and inconsiderate, the Doug that God knew before the foundations of the earth is not stupid or inconsiderate. Stupid is not his identity.

Shame told Doug that he was an idiot, that he was an

addict, and that everyone else thought he was too. Guilt promotes change. It causes us to say, "I did something that violated my values; I don't want to do that again." Shame promotes stagnation and endless cycles of failure. It causes us to say, "I did something that violated my values; I am a pathetic failure."

You may have noticed that the same demon that was heaping bucket after bucket of shame on Doug was also tugging on his wounds and tempting him to numb those wounds with his addiction. I wish I could say this was unusual, but it's not. Usually when I see a demon tempting someone to violate his or her values, I see the exact same demon condemning and shaming the person for falling prey to temptation.

Combating shame can be tricky. On one hand, I have seen many people do what Doug did: internalize shame and take it on as their identity. Shame tells them who they are. On the other hand, I have seen people go too far and throw out their senses of guilt and embarrassment along with their shame. They accuse people of judging them when they are given feedback about how their actions are hurting themselves or others. They say phrases like "This is just who I am" or "I'm just saying it how it is." Though this way of reacting to shame may feel more freeing, the result is still the same. Shame is still telling them who they are; they have only numbed themselves from the pain of it.

I will address this in later chapters, but the only way out of shame is by receiving our identity from God. It is only through hearing His voice that we can separate ourselves from shame and condemnation while embracing His loving correction. His love—a love so powerful that it can require growth yet still love us just as we are—is the only thing that can break the cycle of shame.

SIGNS YOU MIGHT BE UNDER THIS TACTIC

1. Recalling certain memories makes you feel just as guilty as when they first happened.

2. You often feel judged or condemned by others.

3. Anytime you try something new or beneficial, a little voice in the back of your mind says that you are going to fail and brings up memories of failure from your past.

RESOURCES

You may find the following resources helpful if you are under this tactic:

- *The Supernatural Ways of Royalty* by Kris Vallotton and Bill Johnson

- *Unpunishable* by Danny Silk

- *Healing the Orphan Spirit* by Leif Hetland

- *The Gifts of Imperfection* by Brené Brown (Note to readers: This book was written by a research professor at the University of Houston who has spent two decades researching shame and empathy. It is not written from a Christian perspective, but I found this book very insightful and a fantastic help for those who deal with shame.)

CHAPTER FIVE

MAZES

Anyone whom you forgive, I also
forgive. Indeed, what I have forgiven, if I have forgiven anything,
has been for your sake in the presence of Christ, so that we would
not be outwitted by Satan; for we
are not ignorant of his designs.

—2 CORINTHIANS 2:10-11, ESV

THE CLOCK READ 1:14 a.m. as I lay watching my ceiling
fan spin. I had been telling myself to go to sleep for
more than three hours, but my mind was not cooperating.
Thoughts came rushing in steady waves. I chased them
away, insisting I would deal with them in the morning,
but like trying to push seawater off sand, any success I
had was lost in the next wave.

It had been a troubling few weeks. Close mutual
friends were at one another's throats over an issue that I
had almost nothing to do with. I was doing my best to
be supportive to both parties without contributing to the

problem or getting caught in the crossfire. Their conflict was escalating, though, getting ugly. I was sad, but only because I cared for everyone. I was not really involved in the issue, not at first.

Earlier that morning I found out that one of the people involved in the issue had been speaking badly about me behind my back to the person on the other side of the conflict. I found out that this had been happening for months.

My heart ached as I lay staring at the ceiling in a growing puddle of sweat. I kept trying to push the feeling away and convince myself that it was not a big deal, that maybe the person who had told me was mistaken or what had been said was taken out of context. The heat kept rising in my chest no matter how much reason I dumped on the fire of my feelings.

My mind kept filling with images of me confronting my friend, some kindly and others with lots of shouting. I was furious at my friend for betraying me, then I felt guilty for being furious, then I felt furious at feeling guilty about being furious.

Exhausted, overwhelmed, and realizing that my plight was becoming ridiculous, I said out loud, "What is going on?"

Though I had not intended to look in the spirit, I immediately saw a large board appear above me. It looked like a twisted and dilapidated prop from an outdated game show. The edges were wreathed with barbed wire and blinking light bulbs. The board was filled with an intricate maze built from old wood roughly nailed together into slots and corridors. A little cartoon parody of a heart was moving through the maze, its movements frantic and erratic as it wove through a complicated series of twists and turns. A demon hung in the air to one side of the board laughing uncontrollably.

"What is this?" I asked, momentarily distracted from my rampaging emotions.

The Holy Spirit answered, "Where are the exits?"

I looked carefully. The maze was so convoluted that it took several moments for me to run my eyes along its many paths. No matter which direction I took, I found only dead ends and tracks that looped back in on themselves. It was a maze with no exits.

"It's a trap," I said, looking at the maze. "It doesn't go anywhere."

I felt the peaceful presence of the Holy Spirit come over me like a warm blanket. It did not remove the pain I felt in my heart, but it calmed the anxiety that had been tied to it. With this newfound comfort I looked at the maze again, and it all made sense.

I knew that the little cartoon heart represented my heart. I knew the way the heart zipped through the maze was a picture of how I was frantically trying to process my painful emotions. As I watched the heart shoot down one path, stop suddenly, then rush back down the other, I could feel how my mind had been jumping between trying to justify what had happened and being angry about what had happened. As I watched, I could feel the temptation to start running these things through my mind again.

In my emotional turmoil I had been tricked into entering a line of thinking that had no solution. It was an endless cycle of introspection, frustration, and reexamination. I was so desperate to relieve my pain that I did not realize that my relentless attempts to think my way out of it were perpetuating it.

I closed my eyes and said, "God, I don't know what to do. I need help."

It was not my most eloquent prayer, but the results were almost immediate. I watched as the twisted game-show maze started to shake. The nails that held it together began to rattle loose. A panicked expression brought the demon's laughter to a sudden halt. It jolted forward, trying to hold the quivering boards together, but the entire maze quickly tumbled apart and out of sight, taking the demon with it.

The feeling of peace grew. My pain was still there—it didn't even lessen—but I wasn't afraid of it anymore. Suddenly it was easy to talk to the Lord about what to do next.

Since that day, I have seen many people trapped in mazes like I was. Sometimes they look like an endless downward spiral. Sometimes they look like impossibly complex, three-dimensional, ever-shifting puzzle boxes. Sometimes they are drawn in crayon on construction paper. Regardless of how they look, what they do is the same. They bait us into lines of thinking that have no resolution. Some mazes are made to keep us trapped in anxiety, some are made to overcomplicate our decisions, and some are made to make us feel stupid.

As I have stated before, spiritual warfare is primarily a battle of perspective. It is a fight to get you to see your life God's way or the enemy's way. A maze is a trap where every way is the enemy's way.

In the previous story every line of thinking led to further frustration and hurt. I was so lost in my own thoughts and emotions that it took divine intervention to get me out. Even after I saw what the maze looked like and realized that I was being tricked, I could still feel the temptation to dive back into that line of thinking.

Persistent, unresolvable confusion is often a sign of demonic influence, an indication that the enemy may be trying to prolong emotional pain or trick you into making a hasty decision. One of the most powerful ways to combat confusion is to simply stop processing. Stop speculating. Stop wondering. Stop thinking. Stop, take a breath, and invite the presence of the Holy Spirit.

To be clear, I am not suggesting that you shove your feelings under the rug or suppress your emotions. I needed to process what was happening between me and my friends. I needed to decide how I was going to respond. But, more importantly, I needed to see the situation from heaven's perspective.

Seeing from heaven's perspective is not just about getting a direct answer or solution to a problem. It is about engaging with a problem from a place of connection with God. I did not get a solution to my problem that night. It took several nights of processing and reflection to decide how I wanted to respond to the situation. I started each night in a similar state of hyperactive introspection, and each night I halted my internal process until I felt the presence of the Holy Spirit enter the room. Sometimes it took a few minutes, sometimes it took a few hours, but it came every night without fail. He never told me what to do, but His presence made it possible to choose my response from a place of wisdom and peace rather than confusion and pain.

We were never meant to navigate this world alone. Jesus promised that the Holy Spirit would teach us all things and guide us into all truth. When we forget to stop and wait for His presence, we miss out on a big part of what Jesus paid for.

SIGNS YOU MIGHT BE UNDER THIS TACTIC

1. You have a hard time forgiving others.

2. You are frequently reminded of pains from your past.

3. Your thought life is often hijacked by worry, frustration, confusion, or endless processing.

RESOURCES

You may find the following resources helpful if you are under this tactic:

- *Victorious Emotions* by Wendy Backlund
- *The Three Battlegrounds* by Francis Frangipane
- *Cracks in the Foundation* by Steve Backlund

CHAPTER SIX
FEAR

For God has not given us a
spirit of fear, but of power and
of love and of a sound mind.

—2 TIMOTHY 1:7, NKJV

A FEW YEARS AGO I visited an inner healing ministry in the Atlanta area. I shared about seeing in the spirit for a few minutes, answered questions for a few more minutes, and then prayed for some people afterward. The last person who came up to me for prayer was a young woman, and she did not look well.

Her eyes darted back and forth like she was expecting an attacker to leap out of a nearby closet. Her skin was pale and clammy. Her eyes were surrounded by dark circles of exhaustion.

"I need you to help me," she said, finally looking me in the eye.

"OK," I said. "I'll do my best."

"I've been attacked by demons every night for three years. The attacks started happening during the day three months ago. Now they are happening every moment of every day." She took in a few sharp breaths. "And I don't know what to do. I don't know what to do!"

I watched as her eyes widened and her breathing grew more intense. Not knowing what else to do, I looked in the spirit and saw a lampshade on the woman's head.

I stifled a laugh at the juxtaposition between the intensity of the woman's panic and the absurdity of the lampshade; then I looked more closely. Shadows moved across the surface of the lampshade, vague images like crudely cut-out shadow puppets. Confused at why the woman was reacting so viscerally to something that was no more threatening than a children's night-light, I asked in my mind, "What is she seeing?"

An angel that was standing near the woman reached forward, picked the lampshade off her head, and set it on mine. Immediately the whole room looked different. The shadows that had looked small and insignificant from the outside of the lampshade looked massive and domineering from the inside. They formed dozens of horrific shapes that lifted high above me and reached down with clawed hands. Even though I had overcome this kind of attack on numerous occasions and even though I knew that what I was seeing was a trick of the enemy, I began to feel a familiar fear creep up my chest. I blinked and shook my head, and the vision was gone.

I looked back at the woman, who now looked like she was about three seconds away from going into a full panic attack.

"Hey," I said, putting as much compassion into my voice as I could manage, "I know what you are feeling right now. I know how this fear feels. I was attacked this way for three years. But I am telling you that it is not real; it's just a trick."

"No!" Her scream made me jump. "I can see it! It's here! It's everywhere! It's on you!"

"Fear, stop," I said calmly but firmly. Immediately the woman's breathing began to calm.

I have seen people take authority over demons lots of different ways. I almost always prefer to keep it short and simple. Jesus never seemed to spend too long doing it in the Bible, and I would rather not work harder at it than I have to.

"Like I said," I continued once she had fully calmed, "I know how this fear feels. It's exhausting, overwhelming, and seems completely unstoppable."

The woman gave a quick nod.

"But it is also a lie, a trick. It is a lie that the enemy has told you a bit at a time, getting you to believe it a little more each time. The truth is that this fear is nothing. There is nothing behind it. There is no reason for it, other than that the enemy will always take what he can get."

I continued by telling the woman that the goal is not to get rid of the fear. If we just do that, then when it returns, we will be back at square one. The goal is to become so attuned with God's presence and voice that we can feel and hear Him in the midst of fear.

Given my history, I get hundreds of emails from people

who are experiencing demonic attacks, especially attacks of fear. I am stunned at the number of Christians who deal with overwhelming daily fear, especially when I consider how alone I felt when I was experiencing my fear. Fear can be overwhelming, but fear does not always come as explicitly as it did for me when I was young or as intensely as it did with the woman in the story above.

Maybe every time your spouse walks out the door, you picture him or her dying in a car crash. Maybe every time you hear about some debilitating disease, you worry that every sweat bead and skin blemish are early symptoms. Maybe you avoid the news because watching for more than five minutes keeps you up for the rest of the night dreading the idea of strangers kidnapping your children. Fear takes many forms because the enemy does not care why you are afraid; he cares only *that* you are afraid.

I have heard some call fear an acronym for "false evidence appearing real," and while I appreciate what they are going for, this bit of wordplay has never felt very helpful to me. The reality is that people do die in car crashes, people do get debilitating diseases, and children have been kidnapped by strangers. Real evidence is a part of fear as often as false evidence is. Fear is a complicated knot that tightens with every troubled thought and piece of evidence, false or otherwise. Trying to untangle the ever-tightening knot with facts and truth makes sense on paper, but I have found for myself, as well as for many of the people I have worked with, that facts and truth rarely help. The real solution is much simpler.

> You prepare a table before me in the presence of
> my enemies. You anoint my head with oil; my cup
> overflows.
>
> —PSALM 23:5

I used to hate this scripture when I was a kid. I did not
want to sit at a table in the presence of my enemies. I did
not want to see them at all. I was scared to see them. The
idea of trying to sit down and have dinner with my heavenly Father while a bunch of cackling demons sat somewhere off to the side felt like a nightmare. It wasn't until
I had my breakthrough with fear that I realized why this
scripture was so important. God does not want to set a
table in the presence of your enemies because He wants to
test your bravery or gloat at His enemies. God prepares a
table in the presence of your enemies so that you can see
what your enemies look like in His presence.

Whether you experience intense fear like I did when I
was young or some of the subtler shades of fear I listed
above, the solution is still the same: we need to face our
fears while connected to the presence of God. Facts and
truth are excellent reinforcements after an encounter with
God, but without His presence, facts and truth are often
twisted into the knot of fear.

Fear is one of the most common traps that I see the
enemy setting for God's children. Most of the time when I
hear someone say, "I've been under a lot of warfare lately,"
what I usually find is that a negative circumstance or a
series of negative circumstances have occurred and that

the enemy takes this opportunity to dump as much fear on the person as he can. Fear makes us think that those circumstances will never end or that we will never be able to cope with them. Fear makes it hard for us to think clearly and twists facts and truth to its whim. Fear exhausts us with what could happen and hinders our ability to be the conquerors we are designed to be. Sadly, the fear the enemy brings is no more substantial than the lampshade I saw on that woman's head. It is a cheap trick designed to hide the truth.

> Even though I walk through the darkest valley, I will fear no evil, for you are with me; your rod and your staff, they comfort me.
> —PSALM 23:4

It doesn't matter what you are afraid of. It doesn't matter if what you are afraid of is logical or illogical. All that matters is that you know who is with you.

SIGNS YOU MIGHT BE UNDER THIS TACTIC

1. You experience bouts of terror on a regular basis.

2. You worry about something bad happening to your family at least twice a week.

3. You have a hard time experiencing hope for the future.

RESOURCES

You may find the following resources helpful if you are under this tactic:

- *Spirit Wars* by Kris Vallotton

- *Let's Just Laugh at That!* by Steve Backlund

- *Overcoming Fear* by Dawna De Silva

- *Daring Greatly* by Brené Brown (Note to readers: This book was written by a research professor at the University of Houston who has spent two decades researching shame and empathy. It is not written from a Christian perspective, but I found this book very helpful for those who deal with fear.)

CHAPTER SEVEN
DISTRACTION

Therefore do not be anxious about
tomorrow, for tomorrow will be
anxious for itself. Sufficient for
the day is its own trouble.

—MATTHEW 6:34, ESV

OUR YOUNGEST DAUGHTER, Sybil, had just been born. My wife, April, was spending the majority of her time upstairs in our bedroom, resting and bonding with our new baby. Since we had four other children, I was spending most of my time cooking, cleaning, wrestling kids two or three at a time, doing trips to and from school, and occasionally sleeping.

One night, just after I finished putting the older kids to bed, my wife came downstairs. She had been absolutely elated for the past few weeks, in love with our new baby and thrilled at our decision to have one more when we had originally planned to have only four. So, I was surprised to see tears in her eyes as she walked into the room.

"What's wrong?" I asked.

"I'm just disappointed."

"What?" I asked. "You've been so happy. What happened?"

"Not about her," she said, lifting our newborn a bit higher. "I'm disappointed that I went to the antique store."

Confused and still woozy from our sporadic sleeping schedule, I tried to remember what she was talking about. Sybil had been born a few weeks ago; April's sister had come into town the day after to help out. I vaguely remembered them having gone to the store together at some point.

"I shouldn't have gone to the antique store. I took a five-day-old baby out of the house! What was I thinking? That was so stupid. I should have just rested. I only went because my sister wanted to go. She didn't make me go. I went because I felt bad that she came all this way."

"Babe," I said, surprised by the genuine dismay I heard in her voice, "I understand that you regret going. But it's over now, and that was just one day."

"No it's not," she said, her voice growing even more intense. "This is probably our last baby, and I don't want to miss any of it. I spent too much time trying to host my sister. I invited too many friends to come over. We are still too busy. We haven't even picked out her name."

It was true that we had not fully decided on what we wanted her name to be, and I knew that it was normal for April to be bothered by things that were left unsettled. But the frantic way she was speaking and the way she ricocheted from subject to subject felt off to me. So, I did what I always do when I don't know what's happening: I asked the Holy Spirit what was going on.

A demon was floating around April, buzzing and bob-
bing like an oversized insect. It reached forward every few
moments, plucking at something at the back of April's
head. A wispy pinch of material stretched out from her,
more solid than smoke but less solid than silk. I could see
little flickers of warped images on it, as if the demon were
pulling on a movie screen in her head. It pulled one from
the left of her head, bobbed over to the other side and
pulled one from there, and then drifted to the top of her
head and pulled another from there.

"April," I said, interrupting her, "sorry, but I need to tell
you something."

She paused, wiping her face. "OK."

"There is a demon behind you," and I described how it
bobbed and weaved around her head, pulling on what I
now knew were her memories.

"I know that you are sad about some of the choices you
have made the last few weeks. I know that you don't like
that we haven't chosen her name yet, and I know you don't
want to miss out on enjoying our last baby. But that's just it.
All this thing is trying to do is distract you from enjoying
your time with her." I pointed at our daughter.

"What do you mean?" she said, looking down at the
baby.

"Maybe you do need to think about what kind of
boundaries you need with family and friends, maybe you
shouldn't have gone to the antique store, and maybe we
should have already figured out her name by now. All of
those things may be something we need to work on, but

this demon is only bringing those memories up for one reason: to distract you from the very thing you don't want to miss out on. It doesn't care about your boundaries or your sister or any of that; it only wants to distract you. Tomorrow it will probably be trying to get you focused on how guilty you feel for being distracted. That's why it is switching subjects, trying to bounce your thoughts all over the place. It is desperately trying to divert your attention to anything except what is most important."

"So, then, what should I do?" she said, not taking her eyes off the baby.

As she stood there, her eyes fixed on our daughter, I watched as the demon reached for her head again. Its hand stopped short, and it quickly pulled its fingers back and rubbed them with its other hand. It tried reaching for another spot, and again it reared back as if its fingers had been stubbed on something hard. The malicious smile that had been spread across its face faded into a look of frustrated disappointment.

"You just focus on her," I said. "We can figure the other stuff out later. Nothing else is as important right now."

Distractions come in many forms. We can be distracted by entertainment, ignoring personal progress and responsibility for the easy comfort of a movie or book. We can be distracted by our responsibilities, tricked into being so overwhelmed that we become paralyzed with stress. We can be distracted by the future, constantly dreaming into a destiny that we never take a single step toward. There are many kinds of distractions, but they all do the same thing: they trap us in unending loops of worry, speculation, and fear by distracting us from everything God has for us.

Distractions can be tricky. More often than not, the thing that the enemy uses to distract us is not inherently bad. There is nothing innately wrong with watching a movie or reading a book, even if it is purely for entertainment; it is important to be a good steward of our responsibilities; and everyone ought to be dreaming into his or her future. Distractions are not about what we are being distracted with; they are about what we are being distracted from.

In the previous story, April regretted that she had let her impulse to host a guest override her value for spending time with our new baby. That regret was genuine, and she probably did need to take the time to think about why she had violated her values. Her regret was not an attack from the enemy; the enemy was trying to trick her into becoming fixated on her regret. The cruel irony of this is that the fixation on her regret was causing her to continue to do the very thing she regretted—miss out on treasuring the first few days with our newborn.

April did need to work through her regret, just not right away. The best way to fight distraction is not to beat ourselves up for being distracted but to simply focus on what God has in front of us. It becomes so much easier to establish our priorities when we keep God, and our relationship with Him, our top priority.

SIGNS YOU MIGHT BE UNDER THIS TACTIC

1. You are consistently disappointed with where you spend your attention and time.

2. You feel stagnant in the pursuit of your destiny and goals.

3. You experience extended periods of hopelessness.

RESOURCES

You may find the following resources helpful if you are under this tactic:

- *The Three Battlegrounds* by Francis Frangipane

- *Rooted* by Banning Liebscher

- *Declarations: Unlocking Your Future* by Steve Backlund

CHAPTER EIGHT

LENSES

Set your minds on things that
are above, not on things
that are on earth.

−COLOSSIANS 3:2, ESV

I AM CURRENTLY THE director of the Bethel Atlanta School
of Supernatural Ministry. My duties include teaching
classes, designing our curriculum alongside the director
of each year, helping to create a culture and environment
where our students can grow greatly, and planning the
future of the school. One of my other duties is having conversations with students who are having a problem.

Simple problems like missing too many classes or being
late too frequently with homework are usually handled by
one of our staff pastors. Bigger problems like unresolved
differences between students or disrespectful statements
during class are usually addressed by the director of whatever year the student is in. Once a student with a problem
needs to speak to me, his or her problem has usually
grown fairly large or complicated.

One night I found myself going to class with three such conversations on my schedule for the evening. Unsure whether the night would be fruitful or exhausting, I sent a quick message, asking if student number one on my list would meet me during the first break.

An hour later I sat across from student number one, a young man. He looked nervous before the conversation began, unsure of how to fold his hands or whether he should meet my eye. I will not address what the problem was, as it is not important to this story, but as we spoke, his timidity only grew the deeper we got into the issue. He slumped lower and lower in his chair, cringing like I was a moment away from hitting him, giving only three- or four-word answers to my questions.

Now, I don't claim to be anywhere near perfect at confronting people. But this job had given me plenty of opportunities to practice, so I felt that I was at least a rank amateur. My main goal whenever entering a conversation like this was to do my best to treat the person with as much respect and honor as possible. I did not raise my voice. I did not demean him. I knew what it was like to make a mistake, so I tried to address the mistake the way I would want someone to address one of mine: kind but not minimizing or pandering. However, the more we spoke, the more he looked like a frightened puppy.

"Holy Spirit," I said in my mind, "what is going on?"

There was a shimmer, then I saw a grayish film form in the space between myself and the student, making him hard to see. Then an image appeared on the gray film, like a projection on a screen. I saw a life-sized picture of myself, but it was not me.

This version of me was a bit taller, with bigger muscles and thicker features. It was moving differently as well. A slight adjustment of my sitting position translated to an aggressive huff of frustration; a polite smile turned into an angry sneer; and when I spoke, the image of me on the screen turned each word into a threatening shout.

"What's going on?" I asked internally.

"This is what he learned authority looks like," the Holy Spirit answered.

I leaned forward, looked the young man in the eye, and put on the kindest tone I could manage without sounding disingenuous. "Are you worried that I am going to punish you, that you are in trouble, or that I am about to kick you out of school?"

He nodded, his face relaxing a little.

"I just want to understand what happened. After that we can talk about what we are going to do."

After that the conversation went much better.

Later, I was sitting down with student number two, a young woman. I could tell by her crossed arms and the way that she scrunched up her nose that she was not looking forward to this conversation. This time I looked in the spiritual realm right away, and I saw the same gray screen between the student and me.

This time the parody of me that appeared on the screen was more subtle. My polite smile appeared sneering and mocking. A change of posture was echoed as a huffing sigh. Every little move was condescending and demeaning.

"You're not listening!" she said after I repeated what she had just said verbatim. "No one cares about what I am dealing with."

Try as I might, I never felt like I was actually speaking to the student, and it did not get better.

Another hour later, I was with student number three, a woman at least thirty years my senior. I had high hopes for this meeting. She seemed to be sitting at rest, making polite eye contact, and had a kind smile on her face.

Just to see what would happen, I looked in the spirit again and found the gray screen between us. I was surprised to see a slightly younger and more handsome version of myself projected on the screen. I did not know what to make of this until we finished up with the initial polite chitchat and I started addressing the issue at hand.

During the casual part of our conversation, the projection had been mimicking my movements exactly. This changed the moment that I began confronting the problem. My gestures exaggerated into the sly movements of a high-pressure salesman. My smile looked painted on, phony. The projection took on a bored expression whenever the woman spoke.

"Fine... fine," she said, raising her hands in surrender. "I get it. I messed up. Won't do it again. No problem."

I paused long enough to make sure that she was finished before saying, "I am not trying to blame you for what happened. I am not trying to talk you into accepting fault." I then explained how I wanted her to understand only how what had happened affected the school and the other students involved and that I didn't really care who was more at fault. I just wanted to know what she was going to do with the part that she was responsible for.

She looked at me with one eye, sizing up my sincerity, then said, "OK, I guess we can talk about that."

––––––

Lenses are the ways we have learned to expect the world to be. They are how we expect people to act and what we expect them to think. Lenses are not inherently bad; they are a normal part of how we experience the world, but when we do not recognize that our lenses are warping the way we see things, then the enemy can use them to steer us to places we do not want to go.

Our lenses change as we make our way through life, being bent and shaped by our experiences. The previous story illustrates how many of us have different lenses for the same thing. Each student I met with that night had a different lens for authority. The first saw authority as aggressive and overpowering, to be feared. The second saw authority as disrespectful and devaluing, lacking all compassion. The third saw authority as self-serving and manipulative, interested only in your doing what it wants.

Maybe these students had been raised by overpowering parents, taught by disrespectful teachers, or served under manipulative pastors. I don't know for sure, but I do know that the enemy was using their lenses to try to give them a warped perspective of me and to give me a warped perspective of them.

We have lenses for everything, including what is and is not polite conversation at the dinner table, how many times per week close friends should talk, whether you just wave or stop and say hello when you meet an acquaintance at the grocery store, and when it is OK to take the last slice of pizza. As I said, lenses are not inherently bad, but they become dangerous when we listen to the lies that the enemy tries to speak through them.

"Can you believe she said that? Right in the middle of dinner too. How embarrassing! I didn't know she was that kind of person."

"Frank hasn't been calling much lately. I thought you guys were super close. Frank has been out with three other people this week; remember, you saw it on Facebook. He must have found better friends."

"She walked right by and barely even looked at you. You must have hurt her feelings earlier. You're such an idiot."

"Did you just grab the last piece of pizza? What if someone else wanted it? How many have you had already? You're such a pig."

Silly as some of these may seem, these are all examples of the kinds of lies and manipulations I've seen the enemy throw at people. Lies crafted to match our lens of how the world works. Lies designed to sow bitterness, damage your friendships, make you feel rejected, and perpetuate shame.

We can repel these lies by having the humility to remember that we are finite people with a finite view of the world and the people in it. We cannot read people's minds or intentions. Any attempt to do so would be nothing more than speculation. The only way to understand what is going on in others is to ask questions. Asking questions will not only help repel the enemy's lies but also help reshape our lens. For example, "What did you mean when you said...?" "I'm wondering if you are upset with me about something." "I was confused when..." Even though these kinds of questions can feel vulnerable and scary, filling in the blanks with what people have to say helps prevent us from filling them in ourselves with our own speculations or, worse, with lies from the enemy.

Asking questions and operating in humility are great ways to ensure that the enemy cannot manipulate us through our lenses, but healing the broken and twisted lenses that we have received from our upbringing and experiences is a lifelong process. One of the best ways to do this is by developing our communication skills—not just learning how to speak with eloquence and style but being willing and able to pursue understanding and intimacy with others.

That is why I recommend, especially for this section, that everyone pursue the resources found below. They will help you develop these skills. We will be diving into this more in later chapters, but the ability to develop healthy relationships is a fundamental aspect of learning to live free from the enemy's attacks.

SIGNS YOU MIGHT BE UNDER THIS TACTIC

1. You keep running into the same problem wherever you go (every leader is controlling, every young person is disrespectful, none of the churches you go to see you for who you are).

2. You regularly feel misunderstood.

RESOURCES

You may find the following resources helpful if you are under this tactic:

- *Culture of Honor* by Danny Silk

- *Keep Your Love On!* by Danny Silk

- *Brave Communication* by Dann Farrelly (Note to readers: This is an audio/video teaching available at shop.bethel.com. It is one of the best, most succinct teachings on healthy communication I have heard and one of my most highly recommended resources.)

CHAPTER NINE

LIES

We demolish arguments and every
pretension that sets itself up
against the knowledge of God, and
we take captive every thought to
make it obedient to Christ.

—2 CORINTHIANS 10:5

I WAS SIXTEEN YEARS old and at my church on a Sunday morning when one of my friends from the youth group came barreling down the hall, yelling my name.

"Blake! Blake, I need to talk to you right now!"

I turned to look and raised my hands in defense as he skidded to a precarious stop right in front of me.

"I. Need. To. Ask." He said each word with a strained, interrupting breath.

"Maybe catch your breath first."

He waited until his breathing grew less desperate and then said, "I need you to tell me if there is something on me."

"What do you mean?" I asked, knowing exactly what he meant.

"Look," he said, with some of the desperation returning to his voice, "I know you don't talk about demons and stuff. I know you say it doesn't help anybody, but I need you to tell me now, please."

The way he said "please" was so sad that it stifled my refusal. Without further thought, I looked in the spirit.

A small demon was floating in the air between me and my friend. It was thin, had sickly green skin, and was covered in slime. Its back was toward me, and it was wriggling back and forth as it struggled to force something over my friend's head, like a parent trying to dress an uncooperative toddler. It was a crudely made cloth mask. It was the same pea green as the demon's skin, with a piglike nose and mismatched openings for the eyes.

The demon turned and looked at me like it had been caught with its hand in the cookie jar. I immediately noticed that the demon had the same piggish nose as the ill-fitting mask that hung half over my friend's face.

"I mean..." I hesitated, as all my reservations about discussing demons came rushing back. "It's not even that big a deal."

"No," he said grabbing my shirt. "Please, you've got to tell me."

I was thrown off by his mixture of sincerity and desperation. Most people who wanted me to talk about demons just wanted a checkup or their curiosity satisfied. My friend was acting like he had just been poisoned and I had the only antidote.

"OK," I said, "but first I need you to tell me why it's so important. What's going on?"

He let go of my shirt and took a step back, a sheepish look on his face. "I need you to tell me if I'm evil."

I stifled a laugh, seeing how much concern was on his face. "What?"

"Ever since I was a kid, I've just had this... thought."

I nodded.

"I worried that I was bad, that I was evil."

"OK."

"I'm serious." Tears began filling his eyes. "Bad people don't know they're bad when they're kids. They eat candy and sit on Santa's lap and play with their friends like anyone else. Then they grow up and do something crazy.

"I kept thinking about it and thinking about it. Then I started to hear this little voice like a warning. I'd be playing with a friend after school and it'd be like, 'Be careful; you're going to hurt them. Watch out; you're not safe,' or something like that."

I looked at the demon, then at the mask it was trying to fit over my friend's head.

"You've got to tell me." He wiped the tears from his face. "You've got to tell me if there is some demon that's making me bad."

"Look," I said, looking him in the eye, "you are not evil."

"But—"

"You are not evil," I said, interrupting him. "No demon can make you evil. Nothing can make you evil." I then described what the demon looked like and what it was doing. "It's a mask that looks like it. It's trying to convince you that you are like it. It's trying to put its identity on you.

"One of the main things that demons try to do is trick people into associating themselves with a nature that is not theirs. They might throw a disgusting thought at you, give you a weird dream, or tell you that you are evil. But you always have a choice about what you do with those thoughts."

My friend stared past me, pausing for a long moment before saying, "So, it's a trick?"

"A trick," I echoed, "designed to scare you or, worse, to get you to believe it and act accordingly. It's just a lie, plain and simple."

It may at first seem redundant to include lies as their own distinct tactic. All the tactics in this book are rooted in deception. Demons lie all the time. It's what they do. When something you do goes poorly, the enemy says, "You are a failure." When someone is unkind to you, the enemy says, "He doesn't like you" or "No one likes you." Many lies are rooted in truth; they exaggerate or misrepresent something that is true. I included this chapter because it is important to know that though many lies have a grain of truth, just as many are complete fabrications with no truth in them whatsoever.

My friend was beginning to believe the lie that he was evil. It may seem like a ridiculous lie—it certainly did to me at the time—but it felt all too real to him. The enemy had built up evidence by taking every ungodly thought and moment of sinful failure as an opportunity to lend credence to something that was fundamentally untrue—the idea that my friend had no choice but to be evil. The lie was plain at first, but the grains of truth within made it feel more and more real.

So, if some lies have grains of truth and some are just total fabrications, how do we tell the difference? Discerning between these kinds of lies is very difficult, but thankfully, we do not have to at all. Looking for truth in the enemy's lies is like trying to find a penny at the bottom of a barrel of broken glass: painful and not worth the reward. It does not matter if a lie is rooted in truth, has a grain of truth, or is 99 percent true; if the enemy said it, then it will not be helpful to you.

> Search me, God, and know my heart; test me and know my anxious thoughts. See if there is any offensive way in me, and lead me in the way everlasting.
> —PSALM 139:23–24

God is the only one who can reveal the truth. He is the only one who can give helpful insight into your weaknesses, flaws, and failings. God's correction is overflowing with kindness and love; it does not bring condemnation but provides the power to grow. God will bring us truth through His written Word, through His voice, and through our relationships with His children. We do not need to dig through the lies of the enemy to find truth; our Father is the author of all truth.

SIGNS YOU MIGHT BE UNDER THIS TACTIC

1. Condemning thoughts are a regular part of your internal dialogue.

2. It is easy for you to see cycles of failure in your life but not easy to see how to get out.

3. You believe that there is something fundamentally wrong with you.

RESOURCES

You may find the following resources helpful if you are under this tactic:

- *The Supernatural Ways of Royalty* by Kris Vallotton and Bill Johnson

- *The Supernatural Power of a Transformed Mind* by Bill Johnson

CHAPTER TEN
THE TAKEAWAY

I have given you authority to
trample on snakes and scorpions
and to overcome all the power of
the enemy; nothing will harm you.
However, do not rejoice that the
spirits submit to you, but rejoice that
your names are written in heaven.

—LUKE 10:19-20

YOU MAY HAVE noticed that many of these tactics and traps have to do with hijacking things that are not inherently bad. Shame is just a twisted version of guilt and embarrassment, emotions that are designed to let us know when we are violating our values or not representing ourselves to others the way we'd like. Lenses are just the shorthand we create in our minds to help us know what to expect from the world. They become a problem when the enemy tricks us into letting our lenses create a false picture of what's right in front of us. Healthy fear is designed to keep us from eating food that might make us ill, encourage us to drive safely, and make us good guardians of our children. It becomes a problem when the enemy uses fear to torment or paralyze us.

It is important to remember that the enemy has been defeated. Jesus won absolute victory on the cross. The war is won. Light does not have to fight to dispel darkness. Because of this the enemy must use tactics of sabotage, manipulation, and subterfuge. These are guerrilla tactics, sneak attacks designed to turn your own strength against you.

While it is helpful to be aware of what these tactics look like (I would have omitted this section if I thought otherwise), focusing on them too much and spending too much time digging through our lives looking for signs of them is counterproductive. Becoming overly introspective about whether our thoughts, emotions, or fears are our own or the result of an attack can, in fact, be an attack in and of itself, tricking us into shadowboxing ourselves into exhaustion. So, then, what do we do?

A banker friend of mine once told me that bankers generally do not bother with studying counterfeit bills. The methods that counterfeiters use are vast, varied, and changing all the time. Rather than trying to keep up with the ever-evolving techniques of counterfeiting, bankers instead study authentic bills. They become familiar with the texture, bend, and feel of old bills, new bills, and all between. They become so familiar with how authentic bills feel that anything that diverts from that standard is immediately identifiable. They may not be able to describe precisely how the bill was counterfeited, but its inauthenticity is obvious from the first touch.

Real freedom from the attacks of the enemy does not come from familiarity with his tactics but from familiarity with God, His nature, and His ways. Knowing God makes us indestructible.

PART III

BECOMING INDESTRUCTIBLE

We are hard pressed on every side,
but not crushed; perplexed, but not
in despair; persecuted, but not abandoned; struck down, but not destroyed.

—2 CORINTHIANS 4:8-9

LIGHT DOES NOT have to fight to dispel darkness. Jesus
has already won absolute victory. If this is true, then why
do so many people, even Christians, feel like they are in a
losing battle? If dispelling darkness is as simple as turning
on the light, then why doesn't it always feel that simple?

> When Jesus had called the Twelve together, he gave
> them power and authority to drive out all demons
> and to cure diseases.
>
> —LUKE 9:1

Jesus gave His disciples power and authority to drive out demons—the ability and the right to remove the demonic. After His resurrection, Jesus released them to go make more disciples, spreading this power and authority to even more hands.

> And Jesus came and said to them, "All authority in heaven and on earth has been given to me. Go therefore and make disciples of all nations, baptizing them in the name of the Father and of the Son and of the Holy Spirit."
> —MATTHEW 28:18–19, ESV

If this authority and power is available to all the disciples of Jesus, then why do so many Christians feel disempowered?

———

A few years ago, I set up a small children's swimming pool in my backyard. It was less than a foot deep, but it was a fun and easy way to help my toddlers survive the heat of the Georgia summer.

We played outside until late afternoon and then quickly ran inside to get something to eat. All the swishing and splashing had caused my children to work up a monstrous appetite. I knew that leaving standing water was never a good idea this time of year. But my children's requests for a snack were growing increasingly urgent, so I planned to dump the water later.

I woke up the next morning to make breakfast and spotted the little purple and white plastic pool through the window. Chiding myself for not just dumping it out the day before, I decided that I would wait until after breakfast to take care of it. I still was not all the way awake, after all.

The next morning, I spotted the pool again and shook my head at myself, knowing that I should just go dump it out now so that I would not forget. It had rained all night, though, and the grass was all wet and sticky. I would have to put shoes on, and who wants to do that before he has had a cup of coffee?

I could continue to list the days that went by with the pool still full in my backyard and the excuses that kept me from just walking outside and dumping it over, but the number of days and the quality of excuses are both too embarrassing to include here. It is enough to say that after some time, I looked out the window and saw that the water had turned a sickly shade of brown. I quickly walked out to see the magnitude of the damage my procrastination had caused.

I stifled a gag as I saw hundreds of mosquito larvae twitchily swimming in patternless circles, a fuzzy brown gunk forming the background of their revolting ballet. Disgusted by what I saw and frustrated at the knowledge that I could have easily prevented it, I stormed into the house and into the laundry room. I grabbed a bottle of bleach from the shelf and stomped back to the little pool. I dumped the contents into the filthy water and watched as the little larvae stopped twitching.

As my zeal faded, I looked at the now empty bottle in my hand. Effective as my plan had been, I now had a new problem: a pool full of bleach. Thinking that bleach water is probably not the best thing for grass and realizing that I was going to be late for work if I did not get ready soon, I told April what I had done and asked her to not let the kids play in the pool. I planned to figure out how to clean up the mess as soon as I got home.

Another few days went by. Each morning I saw the pool through the window, and each morning I thought of a good reason to take care of the problem later. A few days more went by, then a few more.

One morning I woke up and looked out the window. I saw the same sickly shade of brown in the little swimming pool. Confused and dismayed, I walked down to the pool and found it full of mosquito larvae. The bleach chemicals had evaporated over time, making it so that the mosquitoes could breed in it again.

I dumped all the water out in one big heave, then went inside to get some soap and a sponge.

Silly as the story is, I think it is a fantastic metaphor for how we can understand the nature of the demonic and authority. I had all the power and authority that I needed to instantly dispatch every single one of those mosquito larvae: the bottle of bleach. I used that power. It killed every mosquito. But I did not change the environment that allowed them to thrive there. This meant that after I left, the mosquitoes came right back.

Personal spiritual warfare is not a question of authority

and power. You have the authority. You have the power. Jesus won both for you on the cross. Personal spiritual warfare is a question of environment—not the one you live in; the one inside you.

Demons are rarely the cause of our problems. They are the mosquitoes attracted to still water, the flies attracted to open wounds. All the tactics and traps that I listed in the previous section are completely powerless when they have no place to take root and grow, when there is no suitable environment for them.

Darkness cannot overcome light, but it does not need to if we forget to turn the lights on.

The following chapters are about how we can learn to live with the lights on, how we can build an internal environment that is inhospitable to the plots, plans, and lies of the enemy. These chapters represent the most effective and lasting forms of spiritual warfare that I have seen. They list the factors that I have seen most frequently in the lives of those who live free from demonic attack. These are the things that build a life that manifests the victory of Jesus. These are the things that make people indestructible.

CHAPTER ELEVEN

INTIMACY WITH GOD

*Now this is eternal life: that they
know you, the only true God, and
Jesus Christ, whom you have sent.*

—JOHN 17:3

I HAVE BEEN GOING to church for as long as I can remember. I have been to thousands of worship services and have listened to thousands of hours of preaching. I have served in just about every area of the church, from the parking lot to the pulpit. For a long time I thought that being a good Christian meant that I should go to church as much as possible, read the Bible as much as possible, pray as much as possible, and worship as enthusiastically as possible, all while trying to sin as little as possible. I now realize that I was both wrong and right at the same time.

Relationship with God is the substance of Christianity. It is the foundation of all spirituality. It is the purpose for Jesus' sacrifice, the culmination of the gospel, the bedrock of your life.

Everything you do, think, experience, and believe is

rooted in the quality of this relationship. Knowing what kind of relationship God is looking for, understanding what the terms of this relationship are, and knowing what kind of person you are entering a relationship with are essential parts of getting the most out of that relationship.

I have been married for nearly twelve years now, and still my relationship with my wife is an ever-unraveling mystery. Every day I learn more about who she is and how to love her. I still learn how to do life with her, how to connect more with her, and how to build a bright future with her.

The Bible uses the metaphor of marriage on several occasions to draw a picture of the relationship between God and humankind. I love this because it so beautifully captures the intimacy, mystery, and progression of a relationship with God. We are always discovering more of who He is, more of how He loves us, and more of how we can love Him.

I used to think that the more I read the Bible, the more I prayed, and the more I worshipped, the better Christian I would be. This is true and false. I used to think that the more I got to know my wife, the more we talked, and the more time we spent together, the closer husband and wife we would be. This is also true and false.

Nothing about spending time together automatically makes me and my wife closer. In fact, if I take her on dates because I am "supposed to" or because I think that she will get mad at me if I do not, then that time together is more likely to result in resentment than connection.

Spending time with her builds intimacy only when I do it for the *purpose* of building intimacy.

The same is true of our relationship with God. I have many friends who have built up piles of resentment because their parents forced them to go to church or read the Bible. I have many other friends who go to church and read the Bible out of fear or obligation. They are striving to fulfill the requirements of Christianity.

I am addressing all this because the fundamentals of building a relationship with God, like the fundamentals of building a marriage, are simple and well known. But just as with marriage, I do not want the simplicity and familiarity of these fundamentals to cause you to miss out on the power, freedom, intimacy, and fun that can be found through them.

Nothing is more important in this life than your relationship with God. Here are a few of the fundamental ways we can pursue this relationship and a snapshot of the kinds of things that happen in the spirit when we do.

THE WORD

I walked into a coffee shop late one Friday afternoon, hoping to finish the last few touches on my first book. My first son had just been born, so it was getting harder to find time to write. Happy to finally have a good chunk of time to sit down and focus, I grabbed a cup of coffee and scanned the room for a good seat. My search was interrupted by a wave from a church friend in the middle of the room. I waved back, putting on an

I-am-so-happy-to-see-you-but-I-have-a-lot-of-work-to-do-so-I-am-not-going-to-talk-to-you expression, as I quickly slid into an open seat.

I looked up at my friend once I was settled, wanting to make sure that I had not hurt his feelings. He had a Bible open in front of him with several notebooks, one of which he had already returned to writing in. I let out a comfortable sigh, opened my laptop, and started writing.

After a few sentences, a bright light caused me to lift my eyes from the monitor. As I have said before, seeing in the spirit has been a part of my life for as long as I can remember, so I am usually not distracted by the things that I see. Unless I am focusing on them, spiritual things blend in like faces in a crowd or furniture in a familiar room. They are just part of the background. So, I was surprised when I looked up to see swirling color surrounding my friend, so bright that it stung my eyes to look at it.

At first I thought that it was just an indistinct cloud of liquid light, but the more my eyes adjusted to its brightness, the more detail I could see. Ribbons of moving images, like strips of film all playing different parts of the same movie, were swirling in great twisting braids up and around my friend's head. Heavy drops of multicolored water were falling from the ribbons, like rain seeping through the fabric of a tent. The drops landed on his head, forming into three-dimensional versions of the images on the ribbon.

Caught by the abstract beauty of the scene, I sat for a moment and silently watched the colorful, cascading light.

However, my curiosity soon overcame me, and I walked over and asked my friend what he was doing.

"Oh, just doing a little one-man Bible study," he said, smiling.

"What are you studying?" I asked, looking at what was happening in the spirit rather than at him—something I usually avoid.

"Just Jesus' parables. Reading through them all again, trying to get a better handle on the imagery, how His audience would have understood it, and all that."

I looked down, and for the first time I realized that all the ribbon was pouring out from his Bible. It came out in a dense rush, as if the surface of the pages was an open fire hydrant. It flowed over the table, down to the floor, and up in an arc over my friend's head.

I knew how much my friend loved the Bible. He had graduated from seminary and taught several Bible studies over the years. Looking past what was happening in the spirit, I could see dozens of notes and annotations in the margins of his open Bible, signs of his lifelong dedication to the Word.

Without thinking about why, I suddenly found myself opening my mouth and saying, "Would you pray for me?"

"Sure," he said with another smile. "Why?"

"I just love how much you love the Bible, and I want to love it more."

He laid his hand on my arm and prayed a short prayer. Immediately the cascading flow of liquid light split like the fork in a river and started running up my arm. The ribbons of light twisted around my forearm and ran up my elbow, onto my shoulder, then over my head, leaving a cold sensation wherever they touched.

My friend finished his prayer; it had lasted only a few moments. I thanked him, shared a few moments of small talk, and then returned to my seat. The cool sensation was fading as I went. I started to feel a little silly after I sat down and opened my computer, insecure about how I had burst out with my request for prayer. With the impulse that had caused me to speak now gone, it was hard to remember why I had even felt the need to ask. I had been reading the Bible my whole life. I read the Bible on a regular basis. Why did I ask him to pray?

"Try it out."

I heard the still, small voice of the Holy Spirit echo at the back of my mind.

"See what happens."

"Try reading the Bible?" I asked in my mind.

"Try it out."

I had not brought a Bible with me, so I logged in to the coffee shop's Wi-Fi and found an online Bible. Genesis seemed like as good a place to start as any, so I clicked on it and began reading passages that I had seen a thousand times before.

I read through the creation story, the fall of humanity, Cain and Abel, and the story of Noah. I continued through the stories of Abraham, Lot, Sarah, Isaac, Jacob, and Esau. I made it to the middle of the story of Joseph when someone tapped me on the shoulder.

"I'm sorry, sir; we're closing in two minutes."

I looked around the room and was shocked to find that it was empty. Half the chairs had already been stacked on the tables, and it was dark outside. I muttered an apology and gathered my things into my bag. I glanced at the time as I snapped my laptop shut; it was nearly ten at night. I had been reading for six hours.

The Bible is not a book. It is not a document, record, or set of instructions. It is more. You can read it like a book, review it like a document, study it like a record, or follow it like a set of instructions, and you will get good things out of it. But it is more.

I have loved writing since I was very young. By the time I was in high school, I had read dozens of books about writing. They all had different tips, tricks, keys, and opinions about how to improve one's writing, but one piece of advice was in every book: if you want to improve as a writer, you must read a lot and write a lot. It's as simple as that. In the same way, I believe that if you want to improve your relationship with God, you must read the Bible a lot.

Though reading and writing will not automatically make you a great writer, you will not become a great writer without reading and writing. Reading the Bible will not automatically make you closer to God, but I do not believe that you can have a truly intimate relationship with Him without it.

Every time anyone reads the Bible, something happens in the spirit. I have watched waves of healing water flow out from its pages as a minister reads healing scriptures over a congregation. I have watched the declaration of Scripture release angels to soar through a room, knocking chains from people's wrists. I have watched a single verse send every demon fleeing within a mile radius. I have watched hopes, dreams, and plans for the future form from brokenness and ashes as a young man read the Bible quietly to himself in the corner of a bookstore. Every corner of the spirit realm responds to the Word of God.

Knowing what God has said is the first step in becoming indestructible. If we do not know what God has said, then we are much more easily influenced by what the enemy says. Knowing the truth equips us to recognize a lie.

Because Scripture is so essential, it is important that we protect our hearts when responding to its necessity. It can easily cause some of us to study the Word out of obligation rather than passion. If you find yourself in this state, do not let the trap of shame overcomplicate your plight. All relationships have ebbs and flows, mountains and valleys, even your relationship with God. The measure of your relationship with God is not in whether you have more mountains or valleys; it is in what you decide to do when you find yourself in the valley.

If reading the Bible is boring and stale for you, then make rekindling your passion for God's Word more important than how many verses you read in a day. Find people who are passionate about the Bible and have them pray for you. Listen to sermons by those who have a rich relationship with the Word. Read until you find a verse that strikes you, then stop and carry it with you in your mind for the rest of the day. The Word of God is a living thing. You will not have to go far to find the life in it.

The following resources may help you grow in this area:

- *How to Read the Bible for All Its Worth* by Gordon D. Fee and Douglas Stuart

- *Grasping God's Word* by J. Scott Duvall and J. Daniel Hays

PRAYER

At our church, Bethel Atlanta, we have prayer lines available at the front after every service. This is a great opportunity for our ministry team to pray for the sick, for people who are going through a difficult time, or for people who just want a touch from the Lord.

Just as the service was wrapping up one Sunday, I suddenly had the impulse to join the ministry team to pray for people. It had been a while since I had served on our prayer line, so I jumped up as the rest of the ministry team assembled.

After a few minutes a woman in her midfifties came up and stood in front of me. I introduced myself and asked what I could pray for.

"So, my life is basically a disaster," the woman said with a flat expression on her face.

"OK," I said, pausing for a moment to see if she made any indication that she was joking. She did not.

"My kids hate me. My husband won't talk to me. I have arthritis in both knees and in my right hand, and I just lost my job."

"Oh," I said, unsure how to respond. "That is pretty bad."

"Yup."

"So, you want me to just go ahead and pray for all of that?"

"Sure," she said, her tone growing somehow flatter. "I've done all the praying I can about it, and God hasn't done anything about it yet. Maybe He'll listen to you."

I knew that my prayers were no more special than hers but did not want to argue the point. After asking permission, I laid my hand on her shoulder and spoke a short prayer.

I saw three angels gather behind her as I prayed. Each had a large canvas bag slung over its shoulder. I was wondering what they had in the bags when one of the angels loosened the cinched string at the top of the bag, revealing hundreds of stamped envelopes. They were all different sizes and shapes. Some were clean white, and others were a dull, aged yellow. But all of them had the same small red ink stamp in one corner that said, "Undelivered."

I finished my prayer and looked at the woman. Her expression had not changed. "So, you said that you had prayed about all this already, right?"

"Uh-huh," she said.

"How do you pray? What do you say when you do?"

"I just ask God to fix the problem."

"And do you get an answer?"

"Well, the problem is still there, so no."

I looked again at the bags of undelivered letters. "I see three angels standing behind you with big bags of undelivered mail. I think it means that God has a lot to say to you, but it hasn't been coming through. Have you ever learned about how to hear God's voice?"

"I guess not, no."

I proceeded to give a brief description of the different ways that God speaks. How He does not always speak in plain English and that He often speaks through visions, His still, small voice, and impressions. How creative He is with the way that He speaks to us.

"I'm wondering if you feel so powerless about everything that is happening in your life because you haven't heard what God has to say about it yet," I continued. "Would you like to try to hear Him now?"

"Like, right now?"

"Yeah," I said. "Let's ask God what He has to say about your job situation."

"OK."

I laid my hand on her shoulder again and prayed, "God, what do You have to say about her job?"

One of the angels reached into the canvas bag on its shoulder and pulled out a small letter. As I prayed, the angel opened the envelope and pulled out a single sheet of paper that was covered in golden handwriting, front and back. Before I could read any of the words, the angel tipped the letter over the woman's head as if he were holding a pitcher of water rather than a sheet of paper. The words and sentences on the pages tumbled off the edge, turning to fine golden dust as they drifted down and landed on the top of the woman's head.

"Did you just hear something?"

She was silent for a long moment before she said, "No, I didn't hear anything. But right before you asked, I just felt this sense of peace wash over me all of a sudden."

"That's great!"

"It's nice," she said, "but what does it mean? Does it mean I'm going to get a new job? Does it mean that God isn't worried about me losing my job? Does it mean that I just need to chill out about all this?"

I laughed. "It means that God is releasing peace on you, that's all. If He has more to say about it, then He will give you more."

"What about my husband?" she said, her voice carrying a twinge of emotion for the first time in our conversation. "Can we ask God about that?"

"Of course."

We prayed again, and again I saw one of the angels produce an envelope from one of the canvas bags. The angel pulled another note written in golden ink from the new envelope, but this time, instead of tipping it, the angel laid the note across the top of the woman's head.

"Did you hear or feel something else?" I asked.

"I just had this picture pop in my head, like a memory that I didn't have before." A sudden trickle of tears ran down her face. "It's me and my husband. We're talking and laughing like we did when we first met, but we look like we do now."

"That's beautiful."

"But what is it?" she asked, her tears still flowing.

"I think it's a promise. I think He is showing you what He is going to do."

Three weeks later she came running up to tell me that she had gotten a new job, one that paid even better than her old one. Two months later she told me that she and her husband were renewing their vows. A month after that she said that all her kids were coming over for dinner for the first time in years. After a year nearly every part of her life had been renewed, all because she learned to hear God's voice.

When I was little, I learned to pray before I ate and before I went to bed. I remember lying awake at night thinking through all my prayer requests, hoping that I wasn't forgetting anything. I made sure that I asked for everything as clearly as possible, while at the same time worrying that I was asking for too much at once. I did not resent these one-way conversations, but I always felt that something was missing. I was just not sure what it was.

As I mentioned in chapter 1, when I was twelve, my parents and I started attending a church that was very active about training its members in the gifts of the Spirit, especially prophecy. My mom took me to one of the church's prophetic training classes. That one-hour class completely changed the course of my life.

It was the first time I had ever heard that you could learn to hear God's voice or that He was still speaking at all. This had massive implications for my experience with seeing in the spirit (a story that I have addressed in my previous books), but this revelation had an even greater impact on my prayer life. I was no longer sending occasional requests to a distant benefactor; I was talking with my Dad. I could ask questions and get answers. I could ask questions and get questions asked back to me. I could ask about God's opinion, His thoughts, and His feelings. I could have an actual relationship.

Communication is the lifeblood of any relationship. In communication we can share information, emotions, jokes, insights, thoughts, hopes, dreams, and so much more. With communication we can build true connections between one another. Prayer is nothing more and nothing less than communication with God. And I, for one, cannot think of a more tangible expression of His love than the idea that God would want to talk with me.

Prayer connects us with the reality of God. It familiarizes us with His character, intentions, and thoughts. It helps us experience His presence during trouble and pain. It acquaints us with the authority we have in Him. It builds the foundation of our identity.

Most people would be stunned by the magnitude of the response the spirit realm has to prayer. I have watched as hundreds of angels were released while a young woman prayed for a nation experiencing hardship. I have watched threads of connection weave between broken families as a father prayed for the restoration of their relationships. I have watched a single prayer completely unravel decades of the enemy's plots, plans, and attacks on a man's life in just a few seconds.

Prayer is powerful, but it is the familiarity with God's nature that comes from a lifestyle of prayer that makes us indestructible.

The following resources may help you grow in this area:

- *The Happy Intercessor* by Beni Johnson
- *Red Moon Rising* by Pete Greig and Dave Roberts
- *Translating God* by Shawn Bolz

WORSHIP

A few years ago I was at a conference somewhere in the Midwest. It was being held in a large conference center, with the main auditorium in a large warehouse-like room.

I walked in for one of the evening sessions and found the seat with my name on it near the front, so I set down my things. One of the other speakers was teaching the evening session, and since I had already taught earlier that afternoon, I was happy to settle in and just be a participant.

I had arrived a few minutes early, so I took a few moments to look around as people filed in and found their seats. About six hundred people were spread across the open room, with another fifty or so still making their way in. Each of them had a personal angel—an angel that was assigned to that person for his or her entire life. Another twenty or so angels were running large trains of gold cloth down each of the aisles. I assumed this was in preparation for something that would happen during worship. A dozen protection angels were dispersed around the edges of the room, mostly near the entrances and exits.

Then I stopped looking in the spirit and just looked at the people. I started wondering why each of them had come to this conference: what they had hoped to get while they were here and what had happened in the days and weeks leading up to it. The conference was themed around getting breakthrough. Had these people gotten the breakthrough they came for? Were they here because they were hungry for more of God? Were they here because they were desperate?

Thinking about this made me start thinking about the things I had spoken about during my teaching session earlier that afternoon. I wondered whether it had been helpful to any of them. Had it been the answer that some of them were looking for, or had they been disappointed? Even if I had said something worthwhile, how could one hour of talking really help anyone?

I looked in the spirit again, this time for the bad things that were in the room. This was not something I usually did, but something about my line of thinking had made me curious. I hoped that maybe, by looking at the negative things, I could see whether anything I had said earlier had helped anyone.

About thirty demons were spread sporadically throughout the room, poking, prodding, or pulling on people in one way or another. This was about average, so I did not pay it any special notice. I switched and started looking for soul wounds on people, signs of emotional and mental hurt. Looking around the room, I saw the normal spectrum of minor bumps and scratches everyone picks up throughout everyday life, only occasionally seeing the deep, ragged, and bleeding signs of true trauma. Seeing these things made me sad of course, but the number of people in the room with these kinds of wounds was pretty average too. What caught my attention was that every person in the room was wearing chains.

Some had a simple set of shackles that bound each of their wrists; others were so covered that I couldn't even see them through the knotted piles of metal. My heart sank. Some breakthrough conference this was. Whatever I had said earlier that afternoon must have been completely worthless. Every person was still bound.

I scanned the room searching for someone, anyone, without chains. There had to be someone who had gotten his or her breakthrough. Despair landed heavily on my shoulders. No matter where I looked, everyone was tied up in chains.

You may be wondering why the people's personal angels did not simply break the chains or how a Christian could be so bound in the first place. The answer is simple: angels do not have authority over our choices or our beliefs, and every choice we make or belief we hold has consequences. Those consequences may be easy to imagine with large moral decisions and belief systems, but even our smallest choices and beliefs have lasting effects.

Some of the chains were the result of choices people had made from a place of lust, addiction, or pride, but most were the product of much subtler decisions and beliefs. These kinds of choices and beliefs are rooted in lessons we have learned from our church history, upbringing, and life experience. They are the result of hundreds of little moments—some where the experience leads us to the truth and some where the experience reinforces a lie. Most of these chains were the result of all the little lies from the enemy that people believed about themselves, other people, and the nature of God as well as the choices they made out of those beliefs.

As I looked around at how many chains covered each person, realizing that I had no idea what kind of teaching, counseling, or training could break them all off even one person, the feeling of despair grew even heavier.

Letting out a defeated sigh and seriously reconsidering my career choices, I slumped down in my chair and put my head in my hands. Just then, the worship band struck the first note.

The sound sent a reverberation rattling through my chest. Not the rumble caused by cranked-up speakers and subwoofers but a shaking that rattled my soul. The feeling of despair dissipated like fog fading before sunshine. My discouragement suddenly seemed petty and small.

I lifted my head and looked around the room. People were walking toward the front, eager to engage in worship. Angels joined them, filling all the spaces between the people. Angels and people began to dance and sing together. The angels kept getting more jubilant as worship went on, jumping, spinning, and soon leaping in great twirling bounds all across the room.

The worship team switched to a new song, and all at the same time, each of the angels pulled out a sword. They continued their great leaping jumps, but everywhere they went, they dashed the chains from anyone within their reach. Each angel wore a massive grin as it dove from one person to the next, shattering their bindings.

Soon, the floor was completely covered in broken chains, and I couldn't find one person who was still bound.

The song switched again, and the angels put away their swords. In a cascading rhythm that matched the song, the angels soared, diving somewhere behind the stage. After a few beats, they returned to the room with loads of jewels and golden treasures. They cast the riches into the crowd like toddlers jubilantly throwing armfuls of toys. The treasures fell to the ground, mixing with the fragments of chains.

The band started playing a fourth song, and the angels rejoined the crowd. They ran to the aisles, each to one of the corners of the golden fabric they had laid there earlier. As the music built and swelled, the angels lifted the fabric into the air, flicking the mixture of golden treasure and broken chains into the air. There the chunks of chain and treasure hung, as if the golden fabric had removed gravity's effect on them.

At the start of the fifth song, large gouts of fire began flowing from the stage. The angels leaped forward, fanning the flames with their wings. The fire grew so hot that the pieces of chain and the treasure melted where they floated in the air. The mixture of melted metals began raining down on the congregation, coating them in liquid gold.

Once all the gold had fallen, more angels appeared on the stage and held heavy hammers. They slammed the hammers on the stage in perfect rhythm and perfect unison, sending shock waves through the room. Each wave brought shape to the formless spattering of mixed gold on each person. Metal took pattern and shape. Jewels slowly shifted into fittings. They formed crowns on some and armor on others, but all were unique and ornate symbols of regality.

Worship ended shortly after. As people made their way back to their seats, adorned in new and beautiful symbols of their identity and authority in God, I thought about the discouragement I had felt at the start of the evening. I had felt so powerless, like nothing I could have said or done could have helped anyone. It seemed silly now.

"It's not about what you say. It's about what I do with what you say," the voice of the Holy Spirit spoke, responding to my thoughts.

His words made me suddenly think about the treasures that the angels had thrown into the room.

"That was everything that you said and everything the other speakers have said."

I shook my head, embarrassed at my foolishness and how I had let the enemy trick me into following a line of thinking that led to such needless despair. I had learned a long time ago that I was not responsible for others' breakthrough; I was responsible only to say what the Holy Spirit told me to say. Of course I had been overwhelmed by the chains. Trying to undo the layers of unhealthy mindsets through teaching would have been impossible, even if I had twelve hours to do it. Only the Holy Spirit could take what I and the other speakers had said and form it into something that released as much freedom as I had just seen.

I thought about how the broken chains had mixed with the treasure and been integrated into the crowns and armor that now adorned every person around me.

The Holy Spirit spoke again, and this time I could feel a warm smile in the tone of His voice. "I don't like to waste anything."

I love worship. It is, I think, the most heavenly thing we can do on earth. I have written about worship many times in my previous books. I am still fascinated by all that happens when we worship our God. I have seen moments of breakthrough and impartation like the previous story, but

I have also seen moments of deepest intimacy, times when all the angels leave and there is nothing but us and God. I have seen both emotional and physical healing released in worship, and I have seen people experience the presence of God for the first time. Worship is for God, not for us. But it is revealing that God seemingly cannot help but give us something in exchange when we worship Him.

A mind that is fixed on worshipping God is impenetrable to the lies of the enemy. To gaze upon Him is to put all other things in proper perspective.

Worship is, as I am sure you know, much more than singing a song. Worship is a lifestyle; it is a way of experiencing, viewing, and engaging with life. It is a fire in our hearts that we tend to, recognizing when the flames are getting low and taking the time to add wood to the coals.

Its simplicity is both the beauty and the challenge of worship. Worship is the act of expressing love to God. There is no trick, no three-step method; it is just an act of love. Most of the time, our worship comes from a place of overflow. It is the impassioned expression of excitement and joy. There is nothing wrong with this of course. But if you can cultivate a heart of worship that remains intact whether your life is joyous and overflowing or empty and dry, then you will have the building blocks of a life that is indestructible.

The following resources may help you grow in this area:

- *The Purpose of Man* by A. W. Tozer

- "Worship in All Seasons" by Bill Johnson
  (Note to readers: This is an audio/video

message available on YouTube or at worshipu.
com, a resource overflowing with teaching,
training, and impartation around worship.)

CONTINUE TO GROW

There are thousands of ways to build a relationship with
God. You can go for a walk and talk to Him. You can invite
His presence when you go for your morning workout. You
can ask His opinion while watching your favorite show.
You can ask Him what He's thinking about while you're
brushing your teeth. The point is that when you invite
Him in, any moment can build relationship with Him.

Every encounter with God's presence makes room for
more of His presence, no matter how big or how small.
There is no upper limit on knowing God. He is infinite.
There is always more of Him to know. Whenever our relationship with Him grows stale, it is not because we have
run out of new things to learn about Him; it is because
we have lost momentum in our never-ending journey of
discovery.

This momentum of continuing to grow our intimacy
with Him is the core of becoming indestructible. We are
designed to be hungry for a growing relationship with
God. We grow starving and desperate without it. But with
it, every corner of our lives begins to shine.

CHAPTER TWELVE
COMMUNITY

But if we walk in the light, as he is
in the light, we have fellowship with
one another, and the blood of Jesus,
his Son, purifies us from all sin.

—1 John 1:7

WROTE THIS BOOK to write this chapter. It is not the most important chapter in the book. It is not the most revolutionary. But its subject is the one that I see neglected the most. Community is a fundamental part of God's design for humanity. Connection to other people is not optional. It is not a troublesome complication. It is part of how God has designed us.

Relationship with God is the most important aspect of spiritual warfare. But sadly, many Christians have been tricked into missing how vitally important community is to their connection with God. If relationship with God is the bedrock of your life, then community is the fortress that you build upon that foundation.

Community is not just the place you live; it is the culture that surrounds you, your family, and your friends.

In my view there are three key ingredients to building and sustaining a healthy community. These three things are the solution to 90 percent of the spiritual warfare that I see in the lives of Christians. Whenever someone under demonic oppression comes to me, I ask about these three subjects. Every single time, I find that person is lacking in one of these areas, usually all three. They are friends, fun, and rest.

FRIENDS

A few years ago a friend of mine went through a hard time. His marriage had been shaky for nearly a year, and now his wife was beginning to move toward divorce. He wanted to keep working on the marriage; she did not.

I remember when he came to me and my wife, April, to tell us about what was happening. We had been friends for a few years and done some marriage counseling with them in the past, so we were sad to hear that things were not going well.

As my friend shared his story, I saw a dark figure standing behind him. It was covered in black and rotted strips of cloth from head to toe, and it held a cracked black dagger in its hand. Looking at it put a smothering weight in my chest.

"I don't know what's going to happen," my friend said, with a fair attempt at a smile on his face. "She doesn't want to make it official just yet, so I still have hope."

The dagger trembled at the word "hope" as if it were a vital organ it was desperate to plunge into. The weight in my chest grew heavier.

My friend continued, "I just wanted to let you guys know where we are at and..." He paused for a moment. "I want to pull some of my closest friends closer while we're working through this." He named two other couples and a few of his single friends. "Feels smart."

I nodded.

"So, if it's OK, I'd like to just keep you updated, maybe process with you guys sometimes. And you can feel free to ask me how I'm doing or give me feedback about anything."

"We'd love to do that," April said.

Months went by. I checked in a few times, but my friend's wife was still steadily moving toward divorce. Every time I saw him, I saw the demon too, knife at the ready.

Then, one night, my friend asked to come over again. When I opened the door to let him in, I saw the demon standing behind him, along with six more of different shapes and sizes.

"She is filing the papers this week," he said, after we sat down at the table. "So, there is still a little time for something to change. It doesn't feel right to drag my feet and make the legal stuff more complicated, so I am going to sign if that's what she has decided."

As he spoke the last few words, the demon spat a vile green slime on the knife. Images flashed through my mind as I looked at the steaming saliva: aching loneliness, endless depression, self-destruction, death. In less than a millisecond I saw a rapid-fire slideshow of my friend's life crumbling to pieces. And then the demon thrust the knife forward.

My body jerked, a sympathetic pain rushing through my spine as I thought about that filthy knife plunging into my friend's back. But that is not what happened.

The poisoned knife came rushing forward, then stopped five inches from my friend. The demon twisted and pulled the knife like it was caught in something. The demon got it free, then thrust forward again, but again it stopped like it was snagged in something I could not see. The demon hissed in frustration.

"How have you been feeling?" I asked, keeping one eye on the demon as it continued its futile attack.

He sighed. "Not great. I'm sad, super sad. But I don't know what to do other than pull close to God and pull close to my community."

He continued talking about how he had been meeting with all the couples and friends that he had told us about before, how he had been making sure to talk with God about all the emotions that were popping up during the process, and how he had continued going to see his marriage counselor.

As he talked, I watched as each of the other demons took turns trying to break through the invisible barrier around my friend. A stubby little demon with exaggerated features slammed into the barrier. I felt pangs of embarrassment and shame ripple through the air. A catlike demon with red fangs swiped at the barrier with six-inch claws. I felt the sudden urge to blame and accuse his wife for being the cause of all this. Attack after attack came against my friend. I saw all the horrible destruction that the enemy wanted to wreak in my friend's life, but none came through.

"So, I've been better, but honestly my heart feels good. I'm not mad at her. I'm not really scared. I'm just sad."

The divorce was finalized later that week. I was worried at first, having seen the magnitude of the attack that was coming against my friend. The enemy wanted to send him into depression, trick him into blaming and resenting his ex-wife, or inflict whatever other pain and suffering it could squeeze out of this process.

Rather than let any of these potential attacks set in, my friend pulled his community even closer. He moved in with one of his single friends. He continued meeting with the couples that had been pouring into his life, and he continued meeting with his counselor.

I watched as, one by one, the demons that had set out to perpetuate my friend's pain abandoned their fruitless attack, until only the demon with the knife remained.

I was visiting with my friend nearly a year after the divorce was finalized. He told me about how he felt closer and more connected to God than he ever had before. He talked about how he felt more connected and loved by his community than ever before and that his life had never felt better. He was still working through the pain and was still sad about what had happened, but all that God was doing was more than enough to make it through.

As my friend finished updating me on how he was doing, I saw the demon with the knife stand up behind him. It reared the dagger high above its head, holding it with both hands. The severity of the movement pulled the ragged bandages back, revealing the demon's face. It had sickly gray skin, glowing red eyes, and yellow teeth that were crunched together in a snarl. The weight I had felt the first time I saw the demon came slamming back into my chest. Its eyes flashed, and in them I saw every terrible plan it had for my friend's life and every life connected to his. The knife came down with every ounce of the demon's hate driving it forward. It glanced to the side well before it reached my friend's head, causing the demon to stumble to the ground.

It gave a final shriek so severe that globs of its venomous green spittle flew, sliding off whatever invisible shield surrounded my friend. Then it turned and walked away. I never saw it again.

I weep now as I write this story, thinking of the avalanche of evil that did not come to pass in my friend's life. You would not believe the breadth of destruction the enemy wanted to cause through this single event in his life. He wanted to hurt my friend, hurt his ex-wife, hurt their friends, hurt their family, and hurt each of their future spouses and children. He had an avalanching plan of darkness that would have sent sorrow and suffering well beyond the lives of my friend and his former wife. I saw it all in the demon's eyes the day he left. But none of it came to pass. None of it hurt my friend because when his dark night of the soul came, he pulled his friends close.

Human beings are fundamentally designed for relationship. Even our relationship with God is designed to function best in the context of community.

The Bible is full of passages that encourage connection, friendship, and unity. We are designed to be surrounded by connections with other people. We need mothers and fathers, those who pour into our lives with their wisdom, experience, and insight. We need brothers and sisters, peers to run our race with. We need sons and daughters, people with whom we can share our wisdom, experience, and insight. We need many different types of relationships, but for now I want to focus on the power of friendships.

Ninety percent of the spiritual warfare I see would be completely solved by learning to develop healthy, connected, and vulnerable friendships. This may sound like hyperbole, but it is true. The plans of the enemy disintegrate when they come into contact with healthy connections between people.

The previous story is just one of hundreds of times I have watched a friendship make someone indestructible. I have seen some of the enemy's most devious plans—elaborate chains of lies laid out over decades—be completely undermined by the power of connection to others.

Our relationship to God is our most important connection, but connection to healthy friends is one of the most effective ways to protect our relationship with Him.

Healthy friends tell you when you are acting like less than who you are. Healthy friends pull you out of the traps of the enemy, even when your poor choices landed you in there. Healthy friends will tell you when you are believing lies. Healthy friends protect joy in your life.

Jesus was as connected to the Father as anyone could be, yet He still had friends—multiple layers of them. He had the multitudes who followed Him, the Twelve who were His closest disciples, the three (Peter, James, and John) who were His close friends, and then one friend who was His closest: John. If Jesus needed friends, surely we do.

I know that this one can be hard for some people. It can feel difficult or awkward to start friendships from scratch. Maybe you have experienced pain or betrayal through relationships. It is true that friendships are risky. But living without them is not just a risk; it's a danger. The enemy will use pain—hurt that people have caused us or hurt that we have caused others—to trick us into isolating ourselves. We are never more at risk than when we are alone.

I encourage you to take the risk and look for healthy friendships. I especially recommend the resources I list to help you grow in this area. Having the right tools makes building friendships easier.

The following resources can help you develop healthy friendships:

- *Keep Your Love On!* by Danny Silk

- *Rooted* by Banning Liebscher

- *The Five Love Languages* by Gary Chapman
- *The Path Between Us* by Suzanne Stabile

FUN AND REST

Jim walked into the room with his shoulders slumped and bags under his eyes. Jim was a second-year student at the school of ministry where I taught, and he had just arrived at class thirty minutes late.

His shoulders slumped a little more when he saw me. "Hey, Blake, sorry I'm late."

"It's all right," I said, looking at his exhausted expression. "You doing OK?"

He gave a half smile. "Oh, I'm fine. Work's been piling up. Two guys just quit, so there's a lot more work to go around. The girls have soccer practice two times a week this year. I'm working on my new startup business as well, and I'm finishing up the editing on that book that I've been working on."

"Aren't you guys in the middle of group projects as well?" Second-year students had a three-month-long, student-designed project as part of their curriculum. This could be anything from planning and hosting a large outreach event to creating a website devoted to recording testimonies of healing.

"Yeah, I'm helping out with three of them."

"How's that going?" I asked, feeling a concerned smile spread on my face.

He paused for a long moment, then said, "I think I got it. Just a few more weeks and things should get all lined up."

"All right," I said.

As he walked by, I noticed a small demon hanging off the back of his neck. It was no bigger than a hamster, with pale skin the color of raw chicken. Its mouth was pressed on the nape of his neck, reminding me of the way leeches latch to their hosts.

I see demons on people all the time. Most of the time they are gone in less than twenty-four hours, expelled by the normal process of healthy thinking. When we choose to let anger go and forgive, when we choose to push jealous thoughts away, when we stop and reevaluate our thinking, we remove the enemy's ability to influence us. Demons are opportunists. We eliminate their opportunity when we realign our thoughts to heaven.

Because of this, I am never quick to share when I see demons on people. Mentioning them can often make the problem seem bigger than it is, turning what would have been a one-day problem into something more complicated.

I bit my lip as I watched Jim go, hoping that the next time I saw him the little leech would be gone. I thought I had a pretty good guess about what it was trying to do.

A few weeks later I ran into Jim in the hall again. He did not look any better; in fact, the more I looked at him, the worse he looked. The bags under his eyes had deepened, and his skin looked a little pale. He was slightly bent under the weight of his backpack.

"How's it going, Jim?" I asked, doing my best to sound jovial.

"Pretty good," he said, giving an exhausted smile.

"Yeah?"

"Yeah."

"Is work going better?"

"Oh, yeah, they hired three more guys, so that's much better. It's freed up a lot more time for me to work on my new business. It's going to be amazing." He then took a few minutes to tell me about the software he was developing, things I knew only enough about to nod at the right parts. "I've been coding until one in the morning every night for a week."

"And you're still helping out with three second-year projects?"

"Yeah, but I'm just helping them with some of the tech stuff. It's no big deal."

"And the book?"

He frowned. "Putting that one on the back burner for now. I'll get back to it when the software is done."

I leaned and peeked over his shoulder as casually as I could, looking to see if the demon was still there. The bulbous little creature still hung from the back of his neck, and its pale-pink body had swollen to three times its original size.

"You sure that you don't have too much going on?" I asked, looking at the swollen demon.

"Well, I am pretty busy, but it's just a season. It's how I

like to do it. Push hard and get it all done, then rest after. I'm good."

"OK," I said, going back and forth on whether I should tell him about what I saw. He wrapped up the conversation and headed to class before I could make up my mind. I decided to pray about it. Maybe I would tell him next time I saw him.

Several weeks later I saw Jim burst through the front doors of the school twenty minutes after class had started. Two more demons were following him. One was a spindly, bony creature with dark red skin. The other carried a bucket full of black oil. The leech demon was still hanging from his neck and had grown so large that it nearly hung all the way to the floor.

"Hey, Jim, I—"

"Hey, Blake. Sorry, I gotta go. Late for class," he said, the words tumbling out of his mouth.

"Nope," I said, polite but firm. "I need to talk to you. Please sit." I lifted a hand to indicate a set of chairs in the lobby.

His eyes darted from me to the hallway to the second-year room a few times. Then he finally let out a heavy sigh and slumped down in one of the chairs.

"How's it going?" I asked.

"Great. Look… I'm sorry I've been late so much," he said, his voice still bordering on frantic. "I'm just having a lot coming together right now. Two of the leaders running the second-year projects had to quit the project, so now I'm leading them and building a website for the third project."

"You're leading two projects?"

"Well, no one else wanted to do it."

"And building a website for a third?"

"Yeah, well, I can do it real fast, so I thought."

The bony demon with red skin started jamming a finger in Jim's face, poking him with rapid jabs around his nose and eyes. I could feel the stress starting to compile in Jim. I could almost hear the sound of tasks and duties piling up in his mind.

"And what about your software that you're developing?" I asked.

"We're in the middle of testing right now, so I'm spending a lot of time going back and forth with the testers."

"And work?"

"My boss assigned me to train the new employees, so I'm needing to keep up with that."

"How is stuff with your wife and kids?"

"I mean, they understand. They know it's just a season…" His words trailed off.

The other demon dumped the bucket of black oil over Jim's head. I had seen this kind of attack hundreds of times, so I was not surprised by the look of shame that came over Jim's face.

I could have told Jim about the demon that was working to heighten his stress. I could have told him about the demon that was trying to turn his guilt about how his schedule was affecting his family into shame. I could have told him about the leech demon, but none of that would have helped.

Demons were not Jim's problem. Jim's lifestyle was his problem. The pace of his life had made him vulnerable to stress and set him up for shame. The leech demon was not causing him to overpack his life; it was partnering with his draining lifestyle.

"Jim, what do you do for fun?"

The question seemed to surprise him. "What do you mean?"

"What do you do for fun? What do you do just because you enjoy it?"

He paused for a long moment and then gave me a sheepish look. "Work, I guess."

I smiled. "When do you rest?"

He looked at me like I was leading him into a trap. "I mean, my wife and I watch movies sometimes, and I try to get enough sleep."

"Jim, there is nothing wrong with liking getting things done, but there is something wrong if you are hurting yourself and your relationships in doing it."

He looked down.

"I'm not saying you are in trouble or that there is something wrong with you or anything like that. I'm saying that the way you are living is hurting you."

"I know. I know. I just need to get through—"

"You have been exhausted for two months."

He slumped his head back in his chair as if he were feeling it for the first time.

I continued, "Rest is not just about getting enough sleep. It's about living your life at a pace where you are usually full instead of usually empty. Fun is not just about diversion or amusement. It's about doing things that you love just for the sake of doing them, not because of the results or something you hope to achieve."

I suggested that Jim choose to keep the things that were most important to him but cut things out of his life until he was able to move at a pace where he could protect a lifestyle of fun and rest. He promised to do his best.

I checked in a week later. Jim had told his boss that he was able to train only one of the new employees, passed leadership of one of the second-year projects over to someone else, and put his software project on hold until school of ministry was over.

The stress and shame demons were gone, and the leech demon had shrunk to the size of a loaf of bread.

Another few weeks went by. Jim had started taking his kids to the park every day and took the whole family on a trip to the beach. He had started working on his book again, just a little bit at a time in the evenings. When I saw him after he got back from his vacation, the leech demon was gone.

———

Rest and fun are not optional parts of a healthy life. Peace and joy are both fruit of the Spirit, the manifestations of the transformative power of God in your life. Making time for rest and having fun are some of the most practical and effective ways to protect peace and joy in your life. Peace and joy are essential ingredients to an indestructible life.

Rest is not something we do to relieve exhaustion. Rest is a standard. It is choosing to live the rhythms of our lives with peace as one of our prime measures of success. Peace and rest are not excuses to be lazy or idle; they are the pacesetters that ensure we are able to finish the race. You can accomplish a great deal by living at a restful pace. In fact, you can accomplish a great deal more than you can by living frantically.

Jim ended up completing and publishing two books, finishing and releasing his software, and being promoted in his day job all by the time he graduated his third year at ministry school. He did this by not letting the temptation to live at a frantic pace overwhelm the guiding hand of peace in his life. He accomplished all that he wanted without violating the needs of his heart or the needs of his family. Living frantically can trick us into thinking we are accomplishing more when, for multiple reasons, we are accomplishing less.

Just for fun, let's do a little experiment. Right now, count from one to twenty-six out loud. Time yourself to see how long it takes. Then recite the alphabet from A to Z. See how long that takes. Now alternate between the two so that you say, "A, one, B, two, C, three," and so on. See how long it takes to recite all twenty-six numbers and letters. Our brains are not designed for multitasking; switching between two different tasks takes more energy and slows us down.

It does feel more frantic, though, which can trick us into thinking that we're getting more done when we're not.

Living with rest as a standard helps us recognize when we are letting a frantic pace sabotage our growth and productivity.

Fun is not the same thing as distraction, amusement, or entertainment. Fun is found in activities that we do purely for the joy we get out of doing them, not for the results we expect to get out of them. The Bible speaks constantly about joy being a foundational part of God's kingdom. We cannot hope to sustain joy in our lives if we do not make room for fun.

Fun looks different for all of us. Some of us find our joy in skiing, mountain climbing, and camping. Some have fun with puzzles, board games, and discussing their favorite show with a friend. Some are having the most fun when lying out on the beach with a good book in their hand, playing pickup basketball with friends, or painting a landscape. Fun is deeply spiritual; it protects and nourishes joy.

I have seen so many Christians tricked into building a mindset where they view rest and fun as wasteful and wrong. This is a horrible trap. Living without rest and fun does to your soul what going without food and sleep does to your body: it compiles your exhaustion, creates confusion, and lowers your immune system. Having consistent periods of rest and fun built into your life protects your peace and joy. It keeps your soul healthy and whole and opens your heart and ears to the voice of God.

Jesus modeled this for us. There are several passages

143

where Jesus took time to rest and pray, even when others were making demands on His time. God modeled this need from the very beginning of time. God, infinite and all-powerful, took a day of rest after creating the world and everything in it. He even made this day of rest part of the culture of His chosen people. He also built into that culture several yearly celebrations and holidays, many of which involve numerous days of revelry and fun.

God is the author of joy and peace. These are not just abstract feelings and virtues but aspects of His nature that are meant to be manifested through His children. We cannot fully manifest the nature of God without building a life with room for rest and fun.

The following resources may help you grow in this area:

- *Strengthen Yourself in the Lord* by Bill Johnson

- *Boundaries* by Dr. Henry Cloud and Dr. John Townsend

- *Play: How It Shapes the Brain, Opens the Imagination, and Invigorates the Soul* by Stuart Brown, MD, with Christopher Vaughan (Note to reader: This book was written by a doctor who has spent his career studying the psychological effects of fun and play. Like some of the previous books I have recommended, it is not written from a Christian perspective, but it is filled with

magnificent insights into how God has
designed us to need joy, fun, and play.)

BUILD YOUR COMMUNITY

I was most excited about writing this chapter because,
while other aspects of spiritual warfare are more foundational, these three areas are where I see the most attacks
getting through. These are also the areas where, when corrected, I see some of the most profound change in people's
lives.

God designed us to want and need full and complete
lives. He designed us to need multiple layers of friends, to
need peace and rest, and to desire fun and joy. We are
meant to eat together, play games together, go on walks
together, tell jokes together, cry together, live together, and
dream together. These things give us the opportunity to
benefit from what God is doing in the lives of others and
give out of the overflow of our own relationship with Him.

Community is not something you find. It is not
finding people that like you or people that you mesh with
easily. Community is something you build on purpose.
Community is not just a group of friendly people who have
the right number of potlucks, picnics, softball tournaments,
and Christmas parties. Community is built from the connections you forge with the people around you—connections you choose, build, steward, and grow.

There are tons of ingredients and nuances to building
a healthy and thriving community around yourself. It
is an art, mastered over a great number of years, but I

have found that building friendships, protecting rest, and having fun create an environment for community to grow. Please do not let the enemy trick you into thinking that community is unimportant or of secondary importance. I watch the plans and attacks of the enemy fall to pieces when they come against people with healthy friendships, room for rest, and a value for fun. These three things make room for the light of God to manifest in your life and shine into those around you. The tricks and lies of the enemy simply cannot live in this light.

CHAPTER THIRTEEN

MOMENTUM

So as to walk in a manner worthy
of the Lord, fully pleasing to him:
bearing fruit in every good work and
increasing in the knowledge of God.

—COLOSSIANS 1:10, ESV

KING DAVID IS famous for his intimacy with God. His psalms are some of the most beautiful and poetic pictures of what connection with the Father looks like. David is also famous for his mighty men. They were people from varying backgrounds that rallied around him when he was running from the murderous king Saul. David's friendship with Saul's son Jonathan is also famous, a bond so close that Jonathan was willing to lay down his right to the kingdom for David.

David's life was founded on intimacy with God. He knew how to build a community, both with his mighty men and in his close relationship with Jonathan. David was a great man, a man after God's own heart, but there was one period of his life where he a made a series of choices that were outside his normal character.

> In the spring, at the time when kings go off to war, David sent Joab out with the king's men and the whole Israelite army. They destroyed the Ammonites and besieged Rabbah. But David remained in Jerusalem.
>
> One evening David got up from his bed and walked around on the roof of the palace. From the roof he saw a woman bathing. The woman was very beautiful.
>
> —2 SAMUEL 11:1–2

Most of you probably know that the woman he saw bathing was Bathsheba. David entered into an adulterous relationship with her, which eventually led to his conspiring to have her husband killed, one of the darkest times of David's life.

Though there is a lot to learn from this story, I want to focus on a small part that illustrates an important key. The beginning of the story says that during the time that kings went to war, David stayed home and sent one of his men in his place. David was a warrior king. His victories on the battlefield were as much a part of his relationship with God as his victories in worship.

While David was responsible for the choices he made, regardless of the circumstances, I believe that this story illustrates a vulnerability that I have seen the enemy exploit in others as well as another key to building a life that is indestructible.

And we all, who with unveiled faces contemplate the
Lord's glory, are being transformed into his image
with ever-increasing glory, which comes from the
Lord, who is the Spirit.

—2 CORINTHIANS 3:18

We are being transformed into God's image with ever-
increasing glory. We are designed to live from glory to glory.
We are designed to need forward momentum and growth.

David had lived a glory-to-glory life, thriving even when
he was on the run from Saul. His life had incredible God-
given momentum. I do not think it is a coincidence that
David's biggest mistake happened when he sent someone
else to do what he was designed to do.

You may be thinking, "But wait, you just told me to rest
in the last chapter. Now you're telling me that David was
wrong to stay home and rest?" Here is one of the great ten-
sions of building an indestructible life. We are designed
to live life at a restful pace, and we are also designed to
consistently move from glory to glory. We need victories;
without them it is easy to forget who we are. While I do
not think anything was inherently wrong with David's
staying home from the battle, I think that it is much easier
to forget who you are when you are not being who you are.

Here are a few stories about how we can protect the
glory-to-glory momentum in our lives and obtain the victories that remind us of who we are.

VICTORIES

Years ago, a few years after my wife and I got married, I worked as a sales associate for a medical billing company. I was terrible at it. I made a hundred phone calls a day to hospitals and doctors' offices, trying to get a hold of a billing manager or business manager. During my day I would usually get to the right person four times. Half of the time I could convince them to set up a meeting with one of the senior sales associates to talk about purchasing our services.

One hundred calls, four sales pitches, two appointments: that was every workday.

Sales was not my strength, and I got almost no joy out of the job. But our first baby had just been born, and it paid better than my old job had. The company was still relatively new and finding its overall identity. They changed the compensation structure for the sales team several times, making everyone frustrated and nervous.

Before long, I started feeling depressed and overwhelmed the moment I sat at my desk every morning. Every unanswered phone call felt like complete failure. Every rejected sales pitch felt like a personal attack. Soon, this started affecting my work. I made fewer calls and got fewer sales. Once, for three days in a row I did not make any calls. I just stared at the wall of my cubicle.

My supervisor checked my phone records and confronted me on the third day. He told me that I was better than this. He said that he understood why I was having a hard time but that I still needed to take care of my responsibilities, even if the company was going through a difficult time. He gave me a second chance. He was a kind and good man.

I went back to my desk, feeling like I had just been woken from a daze. For the first time, I thought about looking in the spirit to see what was happening.

I saw a demon in the far corner of the office. It was vaguely the size and shape of a person but bulbous and lumpy. It was covered in piles of fuzzy mold and fungus. It let out a sigh every few minutes as it sat slumped in the corner, sending a cloud of spores into the air. I felt a familiar wave of sleepy depression wash over my body.

Clenching my teeth against the sensation, I slammed myself back in my chair and pulled up my contact list, determined to not let the depression win. I made the rest of my calls that day, pushing back against the heaviness.

I got home that night and opened my computer. I knew that I wanted to write a book about the gift of seeing in the spirit. I had been working on it in fits and starts for years, but something about what had happened earlier that day had put a fire in my heart. I sat down and wrote until I could not keep my eyes open.

I wrote every night for a month, pushing through the depressive wave I felt at work. Soon I started writing during my breaks at work, jotting down a few sentences on a legal pad while I ate my lunch. One day while I was doing this, I looked up and saw a bubble of fire surrounding me in the spirit. I looked over in the corner. The depression demon was still there, its spores still spreading throughout the room, but any of the spores that came near me were incinerated by the bubble of fire.

The company changed our compensation structure two more times, changed what we were selling two times, and then finally went out of business. Despite all this turmoil, I continued to write in the evenings and during my breaks, immune to the depression that had affected me so severely before. I finished and released my first book, *The Veil*, shortly after and was offered a position as a ghostwriter.

People have a built-in need to succeed. We need to be good at something, to contribute to our environment and community in meaningful ways. We need to be significant. While this need can be twisted to trick us into being selfish, power hungry, and unhealthily performance-oriented, it is a God-designed need. The Bible says that we are more than conquerors. We do not feel in alignment with our kingdom identity if we are not conquering.

Many people I meet feel stuck in this area, unsure of what direction to go and what to conquer. There are a thousand self-help books about how to find a career, change your career, or build a business, but while I am sure that many of them have good information, in my experience the best source of direction flows from our relationship with God and is reinforced by our community.

God designed you to live from glory to glory, to be successful and talented in specific areas of life. Intimacy with

Him will reveal what parts of His nature He has placed in you. As the scripture says, it is contemplating His glory that transforms us into His image.

When you build healthy and full friendships, your friends will see things in you that you would have never seen in yourself. They will partner with you and help you find the connections you need to find for a fulfilling, victorious life.

It may seem obvious, but having fun will help teach you what you like. Writing has always been fun for me. Had I not done it for fun, I am not sure I would have known that I wanted to make writing a career, and I never would have gotten the practice I needed to get good enough at it.

Living victoriously is not just about living free from the attacks of the enemy; it is about participating in the release of God's goodness on the earth.

The following resources may help you grow in this area:

- *Victorious Mindsets* by Steve Backlund
- *Dreaming With God* by Bill Johnson
- *Garden City: Work, Rest, and the Art of Being Human* by John Mark Comer

TRAINING AND EQUIPPING

A few years ago, I was at our church, Bethel Atlanta, on a Sunday morning. I had just finished preaching when a man in his midfifties walked up to me and introduced himself. His name was Rob. He thanked me for the message and shared a bit about his background.

Rob had pastored a church in upstate New York for twenty years. Sadly, after his marriage fell apart, the board dismissed him from his position. He lamented the loss of his church, but he also admitted that it had been a relief.

"I mean, you know, we didn't have anything like you have here," he continued. "We didn't have the Holy Spirit, just rules. We didn't have passionate young people like you. We didn't know we could hear God's voice and pray for the sick to be healed." He let out a sigh. "Better late than never, I guess. It's hard thinking about what I could've done with all those wasted years, though."

"You still have a lot of years left, though," I said, giving him a firm slap on the back.

He laughed. "Sure. But I'm gonna have to use them all to catch up to guys like you."

I laughed in return. "I don't know. God's pretty good at redeeming time."

I paused for a moment, noticing that an angel was walking up behind him. He was tall, broad-shouldered, and held a large wooden crate in his hands. A padlock hanging from the front of the crate caught my eye. The keyhole was changing, shifting from one shape to another.

"Have you ever thought about going to our school of ministry?" The words slipped out before I realized what I was saying.

He tilted his head. "I dunno. An old guy like me sitting in class with a bunch of kids..." His words trailed off.

"Old guy?" I echoed. "Sure, there's a lot of young people who go through the school, but we have all kinds of students. We've had people in their eighties go through the school." I shook my head, feeling a little embarrassed. I never pressured people to come to school, but something about the angel made me want to keep pushing. "I don't know, but I think God might have something for you there."

As I spoke, the keyhole on the padlock shifted into a familiar shape: the logo for our school of ministry.

He smiled at me. "I'll give it a think."

I saw him a few months later, sitting in the front row at the Bethel Atlanta School of Supernatural Ministry orientation. The angel stood behind him, crate in hand.

Our school of ministry is a combination of training and equipping. Students learn how to hear God's voice, release healing on the sick, and operate in the gifts of the Spirit. They also learn how to build an intimate and growing relationship with God, discover their identity in Christ, and prepare themselves to be launched into their God-given destiny.

Because every person is unique, every person's journey through school is unique. Part of the reason I have been teaching there for nearly twelve years is because of the joy that I find in watching what God does when people set aside a period of time to focus on pursuing Him. Their experiences are all uniquely beautiful, and Rob's was no different.

During worship on the first night of class, Rob's crate popped open. The angel reached in and pulled out a full-sized, anatomically correct human heart. The heart was beating, but on closer inspection I saw that it was dirty and had bruises and cuts in several places.

The presence of God filled the room like a great white cloud, a response to the worshipping students. I watched as a portion of the cloud swirled down and wrapped itself around the wounded heart. The smudges and dirt were gone in moments, the cuts and bruises shortly after. Within just a few moments, the heart was whole.

The angel walked forward and pressed the heart on Rob's chest. It slipped into his body, disappearing like a droplet in a puddle. Later that night Rob told me that during worship the Lord had been talking to him about what happened between him and his wife. He said that it was the first time he had been able to really pray about it. When it had fallen apart, he felt so powerless, like it was something happening to him that he had no say in. It was the first time he could really feel what had happened and receive the healing God had for it.

A few months later I saw the angel reach into Rob's crate again during one of our prophecy classes. The angel pulled out a pair of glasses and a book. He walked over to Rob and put the glasses on him and set the book in his lap.

We did some activation and practice later that night. Again, the presence of God filled the room like a cloud. This time it moved directly toward Rob and went through the glasses into his eyes. Immediately, the book flipped itself open in his lap, and I saw strands of letters peel off the page, lift into the air, and float into his eyes the same way the cloud had.

Rob came running up to me after class to tell me that he had just gotten a prophetic word for someone else for the first time.

"You know, I had done a class at church one time before and I just couldn't get anything. It was all jumbled up. But this time I saw a clear picture in my mind's eye, and then an interpretation came, just like that." He snapped his fingers.

Soon, Rob was giving prophetic words to his fellow students on a daily basis.

I saw dozens of things come out of Rob's crate during his time at ministry school: a crown that represented authority, a medal that represented the honor the Lord showed him for his years of service as a pastor—many beautiful things. But my favorite thing came near the end of the year.

We were in the middle of worship on a Monday night, and once again, the presence of God was filling the room like a cloud. Worship was especially intense that night. Several students were dancing all across the room, but Rob was near the back, standing still.

Rob was never the most expressive person during worship, so I didn't put much thought into it until I saw the angel move toward his crate. This time he pulled out a short, plastic step stool, the kind you would put in front of a sink so a toddler could reach the faucet. Confused, I watched as the angel walked toward Rob and set the stool directly in front of him.

Worship continued for several minutes with Rob still standing in place. Then, for no reason that I could see, Rob took two firm steps forward. My eyes almost crossed as my brain struggled to justify the difference between what I saw happening in the natural and what I saw happening in the spirit. In the natural, Rob was standing two steps from where he had been. In the spirit, Rob had taken two steps up on the stool in front of him, each step shaving twenty years off his appearance. In the spirit I saw a ten-year-old version of Rob standing on a stool.

As if it had been waiting for this, I saw the cloud of God's presence move and thicken in front of kid Rob. It grew denser and denser, becoming so thick that I could no longer see through it. Then Jesus emerged from the cloud.

I have seen visions of Jesus a handful of times—stories of a few of them are in my previous books—and this time He looked much like He had before. He looked like a thirty-year-old Jewish man, His appearance unremarkable apart from the indescribable expression of kindness and love that shone on His face.

He reached up and held kid Rob's face in His hands and kissed him on the forehead. He stood there for a few minutes, the stool making it easy for Him to stare into Rob's eyes; then He began to speak. Though I could not hear what He was saying, I read Jesus' lips as He continued to stare in Rob's eyes and said, "I love you, son," over and over again.

Natural Rob fell to his knees, tears pouring down his face. Kid Rob fell into Jesus' arms, weeping just as hard. They stayed there like that long after worship came to a close. Nearly an hour later, eyes still red with tears, Rob grabbed me by the shoulder on his way to clean himself up in the bathroom and whispered, "I don't know if I ever really knew that God loved me." He choked on a fresh batch of sobs. "But I do now. I do now."

Rob never came to the second year of school. He and his ex-wife had started speaking again a few months after his first year of school started. They decided to get remarried shortly after Rob graduated from first year and are still married to this day.

One of the amazing beauties and challenges of serving an infinite God is that there is always more. More intimacy. More presence. More freedom. More breakthrough. More. You can build intimacy with God on your own by spending time with Him. You can build community on your own by seeking out connection and friendships. But it is much easier to get more of these things faster when you are in an environment that is designed to train and equip you.

Schools of ministry are not the only places that this can happen. Rob's crate was not full of the things that the school was ready to give him; it was full of the things God was ready to give him. I think the keyhole in the padlock kept changing because there was more than one way to get into that crate. Rob may have been able to access what God had for him in a men's small group, a conference, or a Bible study. It did not have to come through our school of ministry.

The point is that Rob found a place where he could be trained and equipped to grow in his life with God. He chose a place where he would be surrounded by other people doing the same thing. The result was a year that transformed the rest of his life.

The following resources may help you grow in this area:

- *Basic Training for the Prophetic Ministry* by Kris Vallotton

- *The Call for Revivalists* by David Edwards

INDESTRUCTIBLE LIVING

It might be hard to believe that we can truly live an indestructible life. I didn't always think it was true. Over the years I watched person after person get knocked around by the tactics and traps of the enemy, feeling powerless to help. After a while, however, I began to notice that not everyone was affected by these attacks the same way. Demons tried their best to affect everyone, but I soon realized that their attacks just did not seem to stick to some people, even though the demons tried to attack them as much as anyone else.

After thirty years of watching and learning, I have seen that these three categories—intimacy with God, community, and momentum—are the most consistent and powerful ingredients to an indestructible life. Developing intimacy with God is the absolute bedrock of our lives.

Building on any other foundation will leave us less stable and secure. Our community creates an environment that reinforces and protects our lives in Him. Ignoring this, letting the enemy slip wedges between us and other people, being tricked into living a frantic lifestyle, or forgetting that we are meant to protect joy leaves us vulnerable to the lies and attacks of the enemy. Having momentum, achieving victories, and continually growing ensure that we never grow complacent or stagnant. These things build an environment that is inhospitable to the plans of the enemy. They dump the water out of our pools so the mosquitoes do not have a place to breed.

Remember the story from the introduction of this book—the one where a large principality dove down to attack some youth-group kids? That principality was set on causing disconnection and destruction in those girls' young lives. It wanted to get them to hate their parents, become trapped in cycles of apathy and depression, look for solace and comfort in all the most destructive places, and destroy every part of their lives.

Looking back now, I understand why that principality was completely unable to attack those two girls. I remember what their lives looked like. Their parents had invested in building strong relationships with them. They both were deeply involved in our youth group, and they both had been growing their relationship with God on their own. They were close friends with each other and had several other close connections both in and out of the church. They made good grades in school but also had plenty of time for rest and fun. Whether they had done it on purpose or because of their parents' guidance, these girls had built indestructible lives. That principality could not overcome the light that was shining through them.

I want to be clear that indestructible does not mean free of problems and free of pain. Jesus lived a perfect life and still experienced sorrow, betrayal, and pain. Being indestructible helps you know how to avoid unnecessary storms and navigate the ones you must go through. Being indestructible means that you know how to walk through pain with the Lord and you know how to pull on your community to help you get through it. Being indestructible means that you know how to find water in the desert, build a fire in a blizzard, and recognize good shelter. Being indestructible means building a life that is free from the influence of the enemy and rooted in influence from God.

But becoming indestructible is not the end of the story.

PART IV
THE WINNING SIDE

I have told you these things, so that in me you may have peace. In this world you will have trouble. But take heart! I have overcome the world.

—John 16:33

JESUS WON ABSOLUTE victory on the cross. All authority in heaven and on earth is in His hands. This victory was not abstract, not conceptual; it was tangible, affecting, and permanent. Up until now we have been talking about how to build a life that manifests the victory of Jesus, a life that is indestructible to the attacks of the enemy. Jesus won our right to live protected and free, but that is not all that He won.

At the beginning of part 3 of this book, I used a story about mosquitoes in a children's pool to explain how spiritual warfare works. I killed all the mosquitoes in the pool with a heavy dose of bleach, but because I did not change the environment that allowed them to be there, it did not take long for them to come back. In the rest of part 3 we talked about how we can rebuild the environment of our lives to make them inhospitable to the plans and attacks of the enemy, how to change our personal environments.

As I said before, this is the most effective and lasting form of spiritual warfare I have seen. It is easy to see how this is true with personal spiritual warfare since we are in charge of our own internal environments. But how does this apply to the environment around us—our neighborhoods, our schools, our cities, and our nations? How can we hope to change an environment we are not in charge of? How can we hope to have even the smallest effect when so many people, with so many different perspectives, values, and intentions, are contributing to the fabric of our spiritual ecosystem?

How? It is actually pretty simple.

CHAPTER FOURTEEN
WELLS OF REVIVAL

But whoever drinks the water
I give them will never thirst.
Indeed, the water I give them
will become in them a spring of
water welling up to eternal life.
—John 4:14

SEVERAL YEARS AGO, while I was a second-year student
at the Bethel School of Supernatural Ministry, I was
attending a Sunday night service at Bethel Church in Redding, California. A few minutes into the message I suddenly felt the urge to leave, which I quickly recognized as
the subtle but insistent invitation of the Holy Spirit. Trip-
ping over as few feet as possible, I inched my way out of
the row and out the back door.

The feeling quietly urged me out of the building and up
a small hill to a gravel parking lot. It did not take long for
me to see why the Holy Spirit had asked me to come outside. In the middle of the parking lot I saw a fifteen-foot-
tall angel, covered from head to toe in roaring flames.

Angels have been a part of my life for my whole life. Because of this familiarity, I am rarely shocked or overwhelmed by the things that I see. This angel, however, was a strong exception. While its size and the flames that surrounded it were both impressive, what gave me pause was not its appearance but the palpable authority that emanated from it.

We spoke for several minutes, and as we did, I found that it grew easier and easier to see the figure beneath the flames. Like the way our eyes slowly adjust to the sudden appearance of a bright light, my eyes adjusted to the fiery authority that emanated from the angel. He was wearing immaculate and intricate golden armor, covered in beautiful jewels.

We spoke about many things, some of which are recorded in my first book, *The Veil*. But here I would like to address a portion of our conversation that I did not include in my previous account, mostly because I did not understand it at the time.

During our talk, the angel showed me a scroll. Its pages were the dark blue of the sky just after sunset. The angel showed me several things on the scroll, one of which was a map of the United States.

The map was just a simple outline, drawn with bright, crystalline blue lines. Then I saw a small blue dot appear in Northern California, right where I knew Redding was. The dot grew larger and larger, growing into a crystalline blue circle.

A few moments later I saw another dot appear on the

east side of the country, somewhere in the middle of Georgia. The dot in Georgia grew bigger as well. Then similar dots appeared in places across the country, each growing larger and larger until the entire map was the same crystalline blue color.

I knew the blue dots represented something good, but I wasn't sure what they meant beyond that. I thought back to the map a few weeks later when a friend of mine told me that a team of people was being sent to start a church and a school of ministry in Atlanta. Because of both what I had seen and my desire to create an opportunity for others to experience the breakthrough that I had during my time at the school, I joined the team in Atlanta after I graduated.

Two years later I was volunteering at Bethel Atlanta and the Bethel Atlanta School of Supernatural Ministry while working a job on the north side of the city to help pay the bills. One day I was making my daily commute through thick downtown traffic when I was suddenly drawn into an open vision.

Typically, the things I see in the spirit do not override my natural vision. I might be drawn to focus more on them than what is happening in the physical world from time to time, but re-centering my attention on the physical is as easy as choosing whether to focus on the pages of a book or the room around me.

The vision I had while driving my car was wholly different. Though I could still feel the pedals under my feet and the steering wheel in my hands, I could not see anything except what God was showing me. I assumed, since I had no other option, that He would make sure I did not crash my car.

I found myself standing on one of the tallest skyscrapers in downtown Atlanta. To my left stood the angel that had shown me the scroll. After a moment of recognition, the angel leaned forward and fell off the edge of the building, and I knew that I was supposed to follow.

I looked over the edge as the angel fell downward. Though I was completely aware that what I was seeing was a vision, it was still a very long way down. My curiosity outweighing my trepidation, I tipped myself over the edge.

The side of the building rushed past me, the ground approaching much faster than I expected. I plummeted toward the pavement, then passed through it as if it were no more substantial than smoke. I continued to fall downward, seeing dirt and stone rush past me on either side. I fell for what seemed like a long time until, in the distance, I saw a tiny crystalline blue dot. It expanded, growing larger and larger until I realized it was an opening into a vast underground cave, larger than an indoor football arena. The cave was filled with crystalline blue water, a massive underground lake.

I slowed and came to rest on an outcropping of rock that overlooked the lake. The angel was already standing there. After a few moments of silence, I asked, "What is this lake?"

"It is the well of revival appointed for this region." He

spoke in a brisk, matter-of-fact way, but I could feel weight behind each of his words.

I looked out over the lake, watching for a moment how its glowing waters sent rippling blue reflections dancing across the ceiling of the cave.

"So how do we get to it? How do we use it?"

The angel paused for a long moment. Then it turned, looked directly into my eyes, and said, "Learn how to honor."

And then I was back in my car.

———

As the years went by and I started traveling and speaking at conferences and churches around the world, I started seeing something similar in many of the places I visited. When I would drive around different cities and towns, looking in the spirit, I would see crystalline blue water bubbling up from the ground, creating little pools on the surface. I was immediately reminded of stories I had read of the early days of oil speculation in the United States. Oil was so plentiful in some places that it literally bubbled up to the surface.

I began to wonder, If these wells of revival are so available that they are rising to the surface, then what do we need to do to use them, and what does honor have to do with it?

I believe the wells represent heaven's resources to release revival on the earth, the fuel needed to perpetuate the presence, plans, and glory of God. I have heard prophetic words about revival for a long time, words declaring extreme moves of God, nations changed, and a billion souls being saved. I believe these words are true. The previous story and some of the stories in the following two chapters represent my contribution to this prophetic message. But before we dive into what a revival of this magnitude could look like, I want to take a moment to touch on how it is connected to honor.

After I had that vision of the well under the city of Atlanta, I could not get the angel's words out of my head. "Learn how to honor." What did it mean? Honor God? Honor people? Honor other churches? Honor people who don't know God yet? Honor the world?

Years of thinking about this have led me to one answer: yes.

I believe that we are meant to release honor in every part of life: honoring God, honoring people who know Him and people who do not yet, honoring churches and church leaders. I believe that we are meant to honor in every situation. So, what does that mean?

Danny Silk uses this definition of *honor* from *The Business of Honor,* a book he cowrote:

> Honor is all about seeing what's valuable, wonderful, and miraculous in other people and appreciating, being in awe of, loving, acknowledging, and otherwise responding to them in the way they deserve.[1]

My way of saying the same thing is this: honor is seeing the glory of God in someone and responding to that glory. Honor is, in many ways, the practical application of love.

Honor does not mean that you must agree with everyone or approve of everything that everyone says or does. The Bible tells us to honor our fathers and mothers. It does not say to honor them if they are godly or if they are kind to us. It simply says to honor them. Honor does not mean that you cannot disagree with someone, but it does determine the way you handle that disagreement.

Honoring different parts of the body of Christ, as we are encouraged to do in 1 Corinthians 12, ensures that we are all receiving the benefit of what God is doing with His church. Honoring people ensures that we maintain attitudes and behaviors that protect the flow of love between us, even between us and our enemies. Honoring the world ensures that, despite its need for transformation, we still love it the way God does, as He described in John 3:16. Honor protects and perpetuates revival—the unveiling of God's plans, presence, and glory on the earth.

Honor is not something we learn how to do overnight; it is an art whose expression we master over many years. I have spent a lot of time listening to and reading the work of teachers like Danny Silk and Kris Vallotton who have an excellent grasp on the subject, and I encourage you to do the same. Honor protects and perpetuates the glory of God in ourselves and in others. It paves the way for revival. It shines a light into even the darkest places. It is an immensely powerful weapon of spiritual warfare.

CHAPTER FIFTEEN

THE BATTLEFIELD

For we do not wrestle against flesh
and blood, but against the rulers,
against the authorities, against the
cosmic powers over this present darkness, against the spiritual forces
of evil in the heavenly places.

—EPHESIANS 6:12, ESV

SEVERAL YEARS AGO I was ministering at a church in the city of Dresden in Germany. One morning, one of the pastors invited me and my team to take a tour of the city. We bundled up against the cold and began the short trek to the city center.

The city of Dresden was part of one of the most controversial air raids during World War II. It was bombed near the end of the war with incendiary weapons, causing a massive firestorm that reduced most of the city to rubble. The lowest estimates put the casualties at twenty-five thousand people.

After the war there was great debate about whether

Dresden had been a valid military target or an act of revenge for the German bombing of Coventry. Regardless of the reasons for the attack, the human suffering it caused was devastating. The pastor recounted stories he had been told of people desperately seeking to escape, only to be trapped by the encroaching flames.

I started looking in the spirit as we came around the corner to an open square with a fountain at its center. Everything that we do on this earth leaves a mark. Bad things leave a bad mark, and good things leave a good mark. Little things leave a little mark, and big things leave a big mark. I took a moment to look for the mark left by the tragedy of that day. What I saw was simple, but the emotion that flowed through me as I saw it was instantly overwhelming.

The stone streets were impressively clean, but when I looked in the spirit, I saw that they were all coated in greasy black ash. The ash was full of handprints, some big, some small. They formed an eerily beautiful pattern that spread throughout the whole city square. A spike of empathy drove itself into my gut, and I stopped looking in the spirit.

"Many people ran to the fountain here during the fire," the pastor continued. "But the heat of the flames was so intense that the water had already started to boil." He paused. "It was very bad."

We moved forward, continuing toward the city center. He continued his story, saying how the city was completely devastated. Many years later, after the Berlin Wall came down, there was a massive effort to restore the city. They rebuilt all the historical buildings that had been destroyed in the bombing, even going so far as to use some of the original bricks that had survived the fire.

We rounded another corner and came upon a magnificent domed church building.

"This is the Frauenkirche, the Church of Our Lady."

I looked and immediately saw a massive angel standing behind the church. It was at least six hundred feet tall, easily the largest angel I had ever seen. It was wearing nothing except a simple tunic around its waist, but there was a massive blue sword in its right hand. The angel was grappling with an equally massive demon, a smoky-black doglike creature. Each was moving incredibly slowly, barely an inch a minute.

While several things were unusual about what I was seeing, I was immediately struck by how poorly equipped the angel seemed to be. I had never seen a warrior or protection angel with no armor.

Seeing such a massive display had completely distracted me from the story the pastor was telling, but something he said suddenly caught my attention.

"So, when they rebuilt the church, the cross at the top of the dome was made by the son of one of the pilots who had been part of the bombing mission."

"I'm sorry," I said, throwing up a hand. "What was that last part again?"

"Well, as I said, many people believed that the attack on Dresden was an act of vengeance. There was much debate after the war about whether the attack had been justified or not. But years later during the restoration of the city, a son of one of the pilots who had bombed the city made the cross that now sits on top of the church. It was done as an act of reconciliation. They had a big ceremony out here to commemorate the event and the completion of the church."

As he spoke, pictures flashed through my mind. I saw the angel and the demon fighting hand to hand over the city of Dresden. I saw the ceremony the day the church was completed. I saw the blue sword appear in the angel's hand. Then I heard the Holy Spirit speak.

"Forgiveness is a weapon."

I had been seeing in the spirit for long enough to know that the battle between the angel and the demon was not just about what had happened during the bombing. That their fight was happening in such extreme slow motion was an indication of a battle that had been happening for a long time, for generations. The city of Dresden is over eight hundred years old; its history is rich and complex. Even its destruction and reconstruction are a relatively small portion of its history. The battle was over something much larger and much simpler: Heaven had plans for the city of Dresden. Hell had plans for the city of Dresden. The battle was over whose plans came to fruition.

Realizing the scale of what I was seeing—not just the size but the amount of time it represented—I was amazed that the actions of a few people could affect it at all. A simple gesture of forgiveness and reconciliation could leave a mark that affected the destiny of a city.

I have looked in the spirit all over the world. Every place I go has a different history and culture. Every place has different strengths and weaknesses. Every place has different challenges and issues. Every place is different, but something about every place is the same: there are always good things happening in the spirit realm, and there are always bad things happening in the spirit realm.

I have met so many Christians that have a grim view of the global battlefield of spiritual warfare. They say things like "This area is really hard. This area is really dark. There is a lot of witchcraft here." I often hear stories of decades of exhausting work, trying to beat back the darkness. I am so sad whenever I hear these stories of people being tricked into spending so much time and energy fighting a battle that Jesus won on the cross.

While it is true that darkness abounds more in some areas than in others, focusing on that darkness is almost always a distraction. We are meant to focus on the light.

I have two friends who have two different churches in the same city. The city is notorious for its problems with drugs and crime. It has a large New Age community and is known for witchcraft.

One church has spent a great deal of time praying against the ungodly elements in the city and the corruption that has made room for so much crime and drug use. They have protested the local New Age festival with signs and chants. They have run targeted campaigns against city officials they feel are ungodly.

The other church has spent a great deal of time asking the Lord what His plans for the city are. Out of this they have developed community outreaches to minister to the homeless and clean up the garbage in some of the dirtiest parts of town. This opened the door for the pastor to meet the mayor, who soon became a Christian. The pastor is now part of a city council that is planning a reconstruction project to help improve every aspect of the city. He is getting to influence the design of the newly remodeled city center and will soon be running a new community center for youth there.

One church feared their city and has exhausted themselves fighting against it. One church honored their city and has let God show them how to transform it.

It may feel easy to judge the first church, thinking that they are just bad people, but they are not. As I said, the pastor is a friend. He is a kind and compassionate man. He has, unfortunately, let fear of darkness cause him to miss out on the potential that God has placed in his city.

There is no place on this earth where God has not placed the potential for good. I have been to cities with extremely high atheist populations; God was present there just as much as any other place. I lived in postcommunist Russia for three and a half years; God was just as present there. I have been to war-torn slums in Cambodia; God was there. I have been to some of the most stringently religious churches in the world; God was there.

Remember fundamental number two: spiritual warfare is primarily a battle of perspective. This is true in personal spiritual warfare and in global spiritual warfare. The enemy is fighting to get you to see things his way because, as you saw with what happened with a few people in Dresden, even a simple act can release a massive amount of God's goodness, leaving a mark that can last for generations.

Understanding the nature of the battlefield is essential to victory in any battle. If we believe that we are on the verge of being overwhelmed by darkness, then we will fight tooth and nail to beat it back. If we know that God is always ready to do good no matter where we are, then instead of fighting the darkness, we will focus on honoring the glory we see in others, perpetuating the light.

CHAPTER SIXTEEN

THE HARVEST IS PLENTIFUL

*For the creation waits in
eager expectation for the children of God to be revealed.*

—ROMANS 8:19

I DISCOVERED A FUNDAMENTAL problem with Christianity when I was six years old. My family and I were missionaries in Russia at the time. We were living in a high-rise apartment building in downtown Moscow, helping start a church nearby. Russian television in the early nineties was not very compelling for a first grader, so my grandfather, being the brilliant man that he was, recorded children's television channels for me and my sisters and mailed us the VHS tapes.

We watched the same shows with the same commercials over and over again. My favorite show was about a group of cartoon animals that all played together at the same nursery. Each episode was about them playing and imagining together. In one episode they would imagine that they were knights saving a princess from a fiery dragon; in the next they would be astronauts exploring a distant planet; in the next they would be adventurers searching for treasure in a lost city. I remember being so excited when the show came on. I was thrilled to see what their next adventure would be, even after I had seen them so many times that I had them all memorized.

Early one Saturday morning my sister and I sat in front of the TV in our pajamas, eating bowls of cereal, when my favorite show came on. I felt my heart leap with a familiar jolt of excitement, when suddenly a thought occurred to me.

My family and I were in Russia being missionaries. Missionaries tell people about Jesus. The goal, I supposed, was that everyone got to hear about Jesus. Then everyone could be saved. I looked up as the introductory song of my favorite show came to a close and wondered what this show would be about if Christians had made it.

I thought for a few seconds. I guessed that it would be about all the little cartoon animals praying and reading the Bible. I ran a dozen imaginary episodes of this new version of the show through my head, one after the other. Then I felt a stab of dread. The version of the show I saw in my head was so boring. I mean, I liked praying and reading the Bible just fine, but I liked all the adventures the animals had too.

Panicking, I tried to imagine a Christian version of the show that wasn't boring. But no matter how I stretched my little mind, all I could see was episode after episode of cartoon animals reading the Bible and praying.

My six-year-old heart unaccustomed to such violently

clashing values, I secretly hoped that the people who made the show would get saved last; that way it could stay good for as long as possible.

When I was in high school years later, I found myself thinking back to the cute little crisis of conscience I had all those years ago. I now knew that being a Christian involved a lot more than just reading the Bible and praying, but as I reconsidered the conundrum I had found myself in that Saturday morning, I realized the problem was still there. I could not think of a Christian version of that old cartoon show that would be as fun or exciting as the original had been. It should not be boring because God is not boring, but I couldn't imagine it any other way.

The more I thought about it, the more it bothered me. God is *the* Creator. He authored every beauty that art has ever sought to describe. His children should be the most creative and expressive people on the planet. Why could I not imagine them improving on a Saturday morning cartoon show?

And then it hit me.

I knew what the glory of God could look like in a church. I had experienced enough of that to be able to imagine more. I had an idea of what the glory of God could look like in a school. I had seen enough inklings of that to start to picture what more of that would look like. However, I had no idea what the glory of God could look like in a Saturday morning cartoon show.

It seemed silly at first, but the more I thought about it, the more I realized that God did probably have a great idea for how His glory could be expressed through a cartoon. I began to think of other areas of life, trying to see how God's glory could fit. How would it look in the boardroom of a Fortune 500 company? Would it be a bunch of guys in suits, all slain in the Spirit and praying in tongues from nine until five? That sounded fine, but was that it? Or was there more? Was there something even better?

What would God's glory look like in a preschool classroom? A construction site? A convenience store?

What would God's glory look like in the Senate? In the engineering department of an automobile company? In a prison?

What would God's glory look like in the day-to-day life of a family? A homeless shelter? A hospital? A law firm? A hair salon? A veteran's center? A pet store? A bowling alley?

Place after place began running through my mind. Some were so specific and small that they seemed ridiculous at first, but the more I thought about them, the more I began to believe that even if I couldn't imagine it, God had a picture of what His glory looked like in those places.

Rather than coming to a cohesive conclusion, my mind slowly wound down, like a bicycle wheel finally coming to a stop after it's been spun. I had a hundred more questions and no answer to the one that started my wheels spinning.

I sat quietly for a long moment, taking a step back to see where my thoughts had taken me. Ten years of experience and perspective had expanded my view of the problem, but I still did not have an answer. Not yet anyway.

THE GRAVEYARD OF DREAMS

One Saturday afternoon not too long ago, I was out in front of my house watching my kids ride their bikes in circles in the driveway. I was just thinking about going inside to get a drink of water when I turned and saw Jesus at the end of my driveway. Those familiar with my previous books will know that this was not the first time I had seen Jesus, but it was the first time I saw Him like this.

He was more than twenty feet tall, clothed in robes of layered purple and gold so adorned with precious metals and gems that even they were overwhelming to look upon. His head and face were so bright that it would have been easier to stare into the sun, though this did not keep me from trying. My knees shook and I felt small, overwhelmed by the authority that resonated from Him. But I could also feel kindness woven between the emanating waves of power, making it easy to look and hard to look away.

My eyes began to adjust to the light, just barely, revealing that something was behind Him. Tall shelves, so tall that they blocked out the sun, sat in perfectly spaced rows that ran all the way up and down the street in front of my house. I looked closer and saw that each of the shelves was full of large square drawers, about the same size as those found in a file cabinet.

"What is this?" I asked out loud.

"It is a graveyard," He answered, and His voice both rattled my bones and held them together.

"Why is it here?"

"It is a graveyard of dreams."

I looked down the road in both directions. The rows of shelves went as far as I could see both ways, each higher than the nearby trees.

Confused at why thousands of dead dreams would be in a small suburban neighborhood on the south side of Atlanta, I asked again, "Why is it here?"

"This graveyard covers the entire earth. There is nowhere that it is not."

I looked back and saw rows of shelves as far as I could see behind me. Why would people's dreams be piled up in drawers? Why would there be so many? And then a thought occurred to me.

I asked, "Whose dreams are these?"

I felt Him smile, though I could not see it. "They are Mine."

As He spoke, a series of images flashed through my mind. I saw snapshots of other towns, cities, and nations. I saw the rows of shelves and drawers covering every part of every one of them. I suddenly realized, though part of me already knew, that there was no place on this earth for which God did not have a dream. Every city, every home, every part of every society in every country across every part of the world—He had dreams for them all.

With this knowledge still settling in my mind, I looked more closely at the drawers. I quickly noticed that there were two kinds. Some of the drawers were plain, flat gray with a steel handle. The others were beautifully adorned, made of marble and gilded with brass and gold. Some of these even had flowers or ribbons tucked into the handles. Something about the gray ones felt dry, incomplete. Something about the gilded ones felt vibrant, even celebratory.

I turned to Jesus, and He answered my question before it left my lips. "Not all of My dreams come true."

He opened one of the dull gray drawers. It was full of papers, hundreds of them, filling the drawer from front to back. He flipped through some of the pages. The best way I can describe the papers in the drawer is to compare them to a business plan. He had a plan, a dream, and He had accounted for every single detail. He had counted every cost, readied for every contingency, and mapped out every part of every step. It was a perfect and complete plan, but it had not come to pass. It sat in the drawer, incomplete.

He reached down to one of the low shelves and pulled open one of the gilded drawers, just a few inches. I approached the open drawer and was shocked to see feet inside. I tilted my head to look a little deeper into the drawer. There was a person, a whole person, lying on his back.

Again, Jesus spoke before I could ask. "All of My dreams come true through My children."

As these bits and pieces of information began to fit together, I stepped back and looked at the whole shelf of drawers. High at the top of the shelf I saw that most of the drawers were open, while all the ones below were closed. I suddenly realized why they were open. They were waiting for a person to step inside. They were waiting for someone who would make Jesus' dream come true. I looked back down at the closed drawers, and I suddenly realized why

He had called it a graveyard. The closed drawers represented dreams whose time had come and gone. Either they had been completed by someone, or the window of time in which they could be completed had passed and they had gone unfulfilled.

I looked up at the thousands of drawers above and beside me and realized that there were more dull gray drawers than there were gilded ones—a lot more. A spike of fury and sorrow shot through me at the realization. It was sudden and overwhelming. I could see all the good, all the glory that God wanted to accomplish throughout history where none of His sons or daughters stepped up to release His purposes. I could see all the hurting and broken for whom He had laid out plans for healing and redemption, but no child of God answered the call. He had plans for every place on the earth and every moment of history, but so many had passed by.

Without thinking, I whipped my head around, looked at Jesus, and shouted, "Then why do You dream at all?"

He paused for a moment, and the ferocity in my heart steadied. Then He said, "I never stop believing in My children, no matter how often My hope is deferred."

I stood for a minute, letting myself calm the rest of the way. Then Jesus said, "Would you like to see yours?"

I looked up and said, "Sure."

All at once He reached up and grabbed the middle of the shelves and pulled, moving the whole rack as if it were on a slider. The wall of drawers flew by until He slapped down His palm and stopped it.

This new section of drawers was different. Every one of them was gilded, and all of them were open. This was a whole section of dreams that were waiting for His children to arrive.

A drawer sat just in front of my chest. I knew it was mine, even before He reached out to pull it all the way open. The inside was the padding and cloth of a fancy coffin. I was suddenly struck by how narrow the drawer was.

"It seems a bit small," I said, looking down at myself and wondering if my shoulders would fit.

Jesus rested a hand on my shoulder. "That's right; it is small. There's no room for your dreams in there, only Mine."

I turned to look at Him.

"It's all right," He said. "I'll hold your dreams for you."

It was neither a promise that He would add my dreams to the drawer nor a promise that He would not. It was an invitation to trust Him.

Before I could hesitate or think, I stepped into the drawer.

The moment my shoe touched the bottom of the drawer, I was completely blinded by an open vision. I could feel the ground underneath my feet and hear the sounds of my children's bicycle wheels on the pavement, but I could not see either. Though I felt a spike of parental concern, I remembered how, years ago, I'd had a similar experience with an open vision while driving my car. God had kept me safe then; it would have been silly not to trust Him now.

In the open vision I found myself suspended thousands

of feet in the air. I looked down and saw a city far below me, less distant than if I were in an airplane, but only just. I looked to my right and saw hundreds of people suspended in midair just like I was. I looked to the left and saw the same—hundreds of people hanging in the air in a line, facing the same direction.

I looked back and saw Jesus, just as magnificent and glorious as before, floating in the air behind us all. As soon as I looked, the light that surrounded His head spread down, illuminating every part of His body. He grew brighter and brighter—so bright that I could no longer look at Him directly. As I turned away, I saw that beams of light were emanating from Him, thick beams of pure white luminescence. I followed the trails of light and realized that a beam of light was pointed at each person who hung in the air. Then I saw what was happening when the light struck each person.

At first the light split like it would through a prism, bending and revealing all the colors hidden in the white, but it did not stop there. Each of the colors split, bending into more colors, and more after that. They bent further, making oscillating geometric designs of every shape, size, and color, spinning great masterworks of mathematics and architecture. They split more, bending into the organic patterns of leaves, snowflakes, tree roots, and flickering flames, creating massive waterfalls of living and moving art. Again and again the light split into unending forms of color and pattern more beautiful than I had ever seen.

The light bent differently through each person, making each cascading fractal of color utterly unique.

Then I heard Jesus speak again, His voice closer than if He were whispering in my ear. "Look ahead; see what it does." His voice glowed with the pride of a master craftsman revealing a completed work.

I looked ahead, and my whole body went numb.

The bending and twisting patterns of light were soaring out from each person to every corner of the world, changing every place they touched. I saw businesses being started, succeeding, and expanding. Every member of the company, from the greatest to the least, glowed with wholeness and satisfaction. I saw books being written, then turned into films, then seen across every corner of the world. Some represented Jesus explicitly and led people directly to Him; some represented Jesus implicitly and prepared the hearts of millions to recognize Him when they saw Him. I saw churches where signs, wonders, and miracles were the norm. They trained and equipped healthy sons and daughters to train and equip more healthy sons and daughters.

I saw every facet of society, every business, and every form of art, and I saw the children of God who were sent to release His dreams for glory in that place.

I turned and looked to another part of the world and saw pain. I saw sorrow. I heard every voice crying out. I heard every curse thrown out by those who had been left broken and abandoned. Then I felt an impossible blend of wrath and compassion well up from Jesus—compassion at the pain, wrath at the suffering. Then I saw men and women leading armies of people to feed the hungry, serve the broken, and heal the wounded. I saw mothers and fathers running to rescue abandoned children. I saw friends seeking the lonely. I saw hands reaching out to the rejected.

I saw every hurt, every pain, and every sorrow that had ever occurred on the earth and the son or daughter of God who was sent to be His answer.

I saw the plans and plots of the enemy, the culmination of his plans for culture, society, and the people within them. Every one of them dried to a husk and crumbled to ash, powerless in the face of God's unending light.

I watched for hours. The light never stopped. I watched for days. The light never stopped. It only grew as more took their places as beacons of God's glory.

Time went by. I blinked, then Jesus was standing in front of me.

"Is this what is going to happen? Is this what could happen? Your light released through Your people, transforming the world?"

He smiled. "It is already happening."

I thought back to all the gray drawers, thousands of dreams throughout history, so many incomplete or ignored. The feeling of anger began to rise again, frustration at those who would leave God's dreams unfulfilled.

"Stop," Jesus said. The anger vanished in an instant. He stepped forward and rested a hand on my shoulder again. "You decide whether you want to step in. That is all. That is enough."

I blinked again, and He was gone. I stood in my driveway, my children riding their bikes in a circle. I looked at the time. Less than two minutes had passed.

THE LIGHT OF THE WORLD

Light does not have to fight to dispel darkness. Light wins the moment it arrives. Darkness prevails only in the absence of light.

For years I thought about the problem I discovered that Saturday morning while watching cartoons. As I went through high school and college, the breadth of the problem became only more apparent. There were so many places on this earth where I could not picture the glory of God. I was sure that God had a plan for those places—He had to—but I just could not see it. Not until recently did I realize that I do not have to.

What I saw in the graveyard of dreams confirmed what I already suspected: God had a plan for every corner of the earth and every aspect of society. What hadn't occurred to me, for whatever reason, was that He would put so much of His hope in the hands of His children.

I have heard prophecies about a great revival for years, great prophets declaring that a billion souls would come into the kingdom of God. While I have always believed that these were true, I had a hard time picturing how it would come to pass. Until that day in my driveway.

The greatest revival in the history of humankind will not come through the hands of an anointed few. It will be the natural result of the children of God making His dreams come true.

I can imagine what the glory of God looks like only in a few places because those are the places God has called me to release it. I cannot see what it looks like elsewhere yet because it is meant to be revealed by you.

During the open vision, when I saw the light flowing into businesses, schools, churches, and other parts of the world, it all looked perfectly practical. I could easily see the processes, procedures, and checkpoints that would lead to the perfect release of God's glory in each of those areas. Each was shockingly simple and intuitive. The moment the vision ended, I could not remember a single one of the practical steps that I saw. I could remember only how it felt and how it looked in the spirit. This troubled me for several days afterward until I realized the truth: I am not meant to know it or see it until I see it manifested by someone like you.

Every Christian, every one of God's children, is designed to reveal and release His glory. He is ready to release this glory in so many places and in so many different ways that no two of us will do it the same way. God's glory will be revealed through preaching and teaching, but it will also be revealed through movies and books. His glory will be revealed through prayer and healing, but it will also be revealed through business and finance. It will be revealed through discipleship and evangelism, but it will also be revealed through art and design. It will be revealed through engineering and science. It will be revealed through poetry and theatre. It will be revealed through social media, video games, and sports. It will be revealed through music, technology, and government and through every other part of society because He has dreams for it all.

The queen of Sheba saw the glory of God in the way Solomon's palace had been built and the kind of food that he served. There is nothing, no matter how big or how small, for which God does not have a dream.

The plans of the enemy are centered on undermining and twisting the unveiling of God's glory, trapping His children in endless cycles of fear, pain, and doubt. This is the enemy's purpose in spiritual warfare: to stop God's children from shining. But I see a generation of indestructible sons and daughters of God who have built lives that the enemy cannot touch. They manifest the glory of God in every corner of the earth and on every level of society. These sons and daughters will raise up more sons and daughters, who will raise up more. Each will reveal more of God's glory, and thousands will come running to these beacons of light.

You are the light of the world, a city on a hill that cannot be hidden (Matt. 5:14). Jesus said this of His disciples when He was here on earth, and it is still true of His disciples today. You can build a life of intimacy with Him, a deep connection as tangible and meaningful as any other. You can build a life full of powerful friendships—brothers and sisters you can run with at a pace full of rest and fun. You can discover God's dreams and live in the victory and satisfaction of making them come true. You are designed by His hand to release His glory. He is infinite. There is no end to His glory. There is no one in history who can reveal it like you. So, find your hill and go shine.

You are the light of the world. A town built on a hill cannot be hidden. Neither do people light a lamp and put it under a bowl. Instead they put it on its stand, and it gives light to everyone in the house. In the same way, let your light shine before others, that they may see your good deeds and glorify your Father in heaven.

—MATTHEW 5:14-16

NOTES

CHAPTER TWO

1. Robert D. McFadden, "Hiroo Onoda, Soldier Who Hid in Jungle for Decades, Dies at 91," *New York Times*, January 17, 2014, https://www.nytimes.com/2014/01/18/world/asia/hiroo-onoda-imperial-japanese-army-officer-dies-at-91.amp.html.

CHAPTER FOURTEEN

1. Bob Hasson and Danny Silk, *The Business of Honor* (El Dorado Hills, CA: Loving on Purpose, 2017), quoted by Danny Silk, "The Core Value of Honor—Leading With the Father's Heart, Part 3," *Loving on Purpose* (blog), June 14, 2018, https://lovingonpurpose.com/blog/the-core-value-of-honor/.

BLAKE K. HEALY, AUTHOR OF *Profound Good* and *The Veil*, is the director of the Bethel Atlanta School of Supernatural Ministry. At BASSM Blake and his team train revivalists who hear the voice of God, know their heavenly identity, and operate with supernatural power and authority. If you would like to grow in the prophetic ministry, see signs, wonders, and miracles, learn more about seeing in the Spirit, and grow closer to your heavenly Father than ever before, then visit bethelatlantaschool.com for more information or to apply for the upcoming school year.

Your life will never be the same.